Best New Chicano Literature 1989

ტ.უ

Bilingual Press/Editorial Bilingüe

General Editor
   Gary D. Keller

Managing Editor
   Karen S. Van Hooft

Senior Editor
   Mary M. Keller

Assistant Editor
   Linda St. George Thurston

Editorial Board
   Juan Goytisolo
   Francisco Jiménez
   Eduardo Rivera
   Severo Sarduy
   Mario Vargas Llosa

Address:
Bilingual Review/Press
Hispanic Research Center
Arizona State University
Tempe, Arizona 85287
(602) 965-3867

Best New Chicano Literature 1989

Edited by
Julian Palley

University of California, Irvine

Cenzontle:
Anthologies Nos. 10 and 11

Bilingual Press/Editorial Bilingüe
TEMPE, ARIZONA

ISBN: 0-927534-01-0

PRINTED IN THE UNITED STATES OF AMERICA

Cover design by Christopher J. Bidlack

Acknowledgments

The editors gratefully acknowledge a grant from the School of Humanities,
University of California, Irvine, in partial support of the publication of this
volume.

This volume is also supported by a grant from the National Endowment for the
Arts in Washington, D.C., a Federal agency.

The editors acknowledge the prior appearance of some of the poems and stories
included here in the following publications:

"Curve Ball" and "House Calls on 15th Street" by Andrea Teresa Arenas, in
Nosotras: Latina Literature Today, eds. María del Carmen Boza, Beverly Silva,
and Carmen Valle (Bilingual Press, 1986)
"The Raza Who Scored Big in Anáhuac" by Gary D. Keller, in *Tales of El
Huitlacoche* (Colorado Springs: Maize Press, 1984).

Contents

Preface

This new collection—the winners of the 10th and 11th Chicano Literary Contests held at the University of California, Irvine—offers a variety of forms of viewing the Mexican-American experience in these last decades of the twentieth century. The ironic "Grus Xicanus" creates a new migratory bird with cosmological ambitions. The humorous modes of "Memoir: Checker-Piece," "Payback," and "The Raza Who Scored Big in Anáhuac" explore the under- and overside of the barrio as well as (in the last-mentioned story) recounting the bewildering adventures of a carnal cast into the maze of his ancestral Mexico City. "Shadows on Ebbing Water" depicts in more universal terms the tragic outcome of a love gone awry, while "Sunland" fantasizes the final days of a woman in a nursing home. Deborah Fernández Badillo and Andrea Teresa Arenas are two feminist poets whose sharp and witty eyes take in the tragicomic scene of their personal and social lives. Francisco X. Alarcón's poetry combines a self-deprecatory humor with a terse, telegraphic style. David Nava Monreal, Rosalinda Hernández, Víctor Avila, and Juan Delgado, each in his or her own manner, focus on a moment of life lived between two cultures.

May these poems and stories go forth and find their readers on both sides of the borders—literal and figurative—that separate and unite us. Perhaps some skeptical Virginia may discover that there is, indeed, a Chicano literature out there, one that will take an honored place among those regional and ethnic expressions to which we give the multifaceted name of American literature.

We would like to dedicate this anthology to the memory of Tomás Rivera (1935-1984), a fine novelist and splendid human being.

JULIAN PALLEY

Note: The 10th and 11th Awards Ceremonies took place during the month of May in 1984 and 1985.

Award Winners

POETRY

10th Contest:

First Place:	Francisco X. Alarcón, "Tattoos"
Second Place:	Víctor Avila, "Outside of Eden"
	Andrea Teresa Arenas, "Poems"
Third Place:	Juan Delgado, "Landscapes"
	David Nava Monreal, "Variations Between Worlds"

11th Contest:

First Place:	Deborah Fernández Badillo, "Poems"
Second Place:	Rosalinda Hernández, "Poems"

SHORT STORY

10th Contest:

First Place:	Lucha Corpi, "Shadows on Ebbing Water"
Second Place:	Michael Ricardo, "Grus Xicanus"
Third Place:	Patricio F. Vargas, "Payback"
	Ana María Salazar, "La última despedida"
Honorable Mention:	El Huitlacoche, "The Raza Who Scored Big in Anáhuac"

11th Contest:

Second Place:	Juan Felipe Herrera, "Memoir: Checker-Piece"
	Margarita Luna Robles, "Urbano: Letters of the Horseshoe Murder"
Third Place:	Gloria Velásquez Treviño, "Sunland"
	Fausto Avendaño, "Los buenos indicios"

Poems

Deborah Fernández Badillo

PINCHED TOES

At the start of the day
I yelled at little Benjie for spilling his cereal,
then I pulled Gloria's hair too hard when it wouldn't
twist into an even braid

Baby Lala got on my nerves for wetting her diaper
twice before breakfast *and* for spitting up her rice
and milk all over my last clean dress

and let's not even think about last night

I didn't want to kiss Rudy at all this morning
because of the way he asked if there was any
fresh tortillas and could I make a better lunch today
cuz he was getting tired of how I made his sandwiches

not to mention that the man still can't find
his own clean clothes and it's because
they are nesting under last week's calzones

And if Josie wants me to watch her little pack of
animals again I'm gonna sell 'em to the Circus Vargas

I'm gonna bite the dog too

I hate K-MART shoes

SOLTERA

The rain is a quiet whisper in my ears tonight
si quería
I could shatter soltera and dance in the rainlight
desnuda

and tonight

when soft July slips through the tiny holes of my
window screen I will call for violin and angels
and dance with God because He is the only he

remaining

and tonight

I lower my bird self onto the thinly carpeted
floor under my bed and pedal an
invisible bicycle until I scream and curse
the He and the he because my legs no longer
fill with blood

because my heart has failed me

Terror Eyes

Tina
used to dance to the Four Tops with that shaky
little hip-step she made up one morning while we
stayed home from school and glittered our fingernails

we used to go out with the same boys
sharing them on a rotating basis
we wore gold earrings dark lipstick black heels

great for dancing
and Tina would laugh forever on account of her
joyous disposition and the night air

sometimes we had to hold our breaths for about
a month and a half before we could breathe again
but it was always worth it.

I don't visit or call or in any way communicate
with Tina anymore, not since her husband
showed me the damp narrow tunnels in his eyes

he wanted me to understand something about how
a man has needs and desires that have nothing to do
with nothing at all

except no job no money no self-respect or
some such foolish thing, I saw his plan of action
and what is there to do but reject the

heroic rapist and draw yourself away from the
crocodile who cries himself a river
because you have seen the poisoned shadows in his eyes.

Last time I saw Tina she wore dark glasses
that didn't cover her purple eyes or blue cheek
and there really isn't any way to hide a broken arm

she ran away from me
so after I washed my dishes all I could do was
light three candles and remember

Tina used to dance to the Four Tops with that
shaky little hip-step and laugh until forever
with the coming of the dawn.

Tattoos

Francisco X. Alarcón

poems
fill up
pages

tattoos
puncture
flesh

DREAMS OF A CALIFORNIAN POET
IN PRISON

*After Derra Caulk in About Time: An Anthology
of California Prison Writing (1980)*

each morning
I wake up
alone
pretending

that my arm
is the flesh
of your body
pressing

against my lips

SUEÑOS DE UN POETA DE CALIFORNIA
EN PRISIÓN

cada mañana
me despierto
solo
fingiendo

que mi brazo
es la carne
de tu cuerpo
pesando

sobre mis labios

RAÍCES

mis raíces
las cargo
siempre
conmigo
enrolladas
me sirven
de almohada

ROOTS

I carry
my roots
with me
all the time
rolled up
I use them
as my pillow

So Real

everything has been so real
the chairs   the doors
so chairlike   so doorlike
the sun has not skipped
a single day
nights have come after days
& days after nights
so daylike   so nightlike
everything so real & so certain
like my hands   your hands
your lips & mine
so fleshlike   so bloodlike
everything so really certain
& so certainly real
everything   even this voice
that sometimes deep
inside feels itself
so uncertain   so unreal

Tan real

todo ha sido tan real
las sillas   las puertas
tan sillas   tan puertas
ni un solo día
se ha saltado el sol
las noches han seguido
a los días
y los días a las noches
tan días   tan noches
todo tan real y tan cierto
como mis manos   tus manos

tus labios y los míos
tan carne   tan sangre
todo tan realmente cierto
y tan ciertamente real
todo   aun esta voz que a veces
en el fondo se sabe
tan incierta   tan irreal

CURRICULUM VITAE

weaknesses are my strength
streets my university
poverty my wealth
trees my kind of books
despair my most sincere
hope
vices my virtue
earth my heaven
& la locura de esta vida
my only wisdom

LUZ

teñida de noche
tengo la piel
en este país
de mediodía
pero más oscura
tengo el alma
de tanta luz
que llevo adentro

"DARK"

I used to be
much
   much
      darker
dark
as la tierra
recién llovida

dark
was all
I ever wanted
I would sing
dark
dream dark
talk only dark

happiness
was to spend
whole
afternoons
tirado
como foca
bajo el sol

"you're already
so dark
muy prieto
too indio!"
some would lash
at my happy
darkness

now
I'm not as dark
quizás
sean los años
maybe
I'm too far
up north

anyway here
"dark"
is only
for the ashes:
the stuff
lonely nights
are made of

FLAGS

stupid
rags
soaked
in blood

BANDERAS

trapos
imbéciles
empapados
en sangre

PATRIA

nosotros
los que nacimos
marcados
de extranjeros
en nuestra propia
tierra
los que pagamos
con moneda dura
hasta por este aire
que nos raja y niega
los que regalamos
todo lo que todavía
no nos roban

nosotros
los que nada poseemos
los reducidos
a sombras
los que llevamos
en los ojos
una noche cruel
y oscura
sólo nos reconocemos
en las estrellas:
sabemos que nuestra
patria
está por hacerse

GUERRA FLORIDA

we opened   we gave them
the doors   all the fruits
of our homes   of this land
to greet them   they poisoned
they came in   with silvery
& evicted us   mercury
we showed them   our rivers
the open green   our veins
of our valleys   but we survived
the clear blue   the slaughter
of the sky   of our days
they cut down   now we face them
the forests   in this final
for their furnaces   battle
for their crosses   for our lives

desert
give us
your endurance
mountains
grant us
your strength
wind
blow us
some courage
madre agua
guide us
in your flowering
& victorious
ways

brothers
& sisters
don't be afraid
the flowers
the feathers
are
on our side

A MI CAMA

ésta es la humilde balsa
en que navego
todas las noches
buscando salvar los restos
de un naufragio olvidado

éste es el pequeño solar
donde planto
las semillas mágicas
de mis sueños que pretenden
las estrellas

éste es el muelle
de un puerto pobre
que con ansias espera
que del horizonte regresen
los mineros

ésta es mi isla perdida
mi pedazo de cielo
mi ruedo   mi alberca
mi cuadrilátero
lo que me queda de árabe

ésta es la mesa tendida
y rodeada de ángeles
mi último refugio
mi tumba   mi nido
mi valle
el verdadero altar
de mi templo
bendita seas
cama

TO MY BED

this is the humble raft
on which I sail
through the night
trying to salvage the remains
of a forgotten shipwreck

this is the small pot
where I sow
the magic seeds
of my dreams longing
for the stars

this is the docking pier
of a poverty-stricken port
anxiously waiting for
the sailors' return
over the horizon

this is my missing island
my piece of heaven
my arena   my swimming pool
my wrestling ring
what's left of the Arab in me

this is the table tended
& surrounded by angels
my ultimate shelter
my grave   my nest
my valley
the true altar
of my temple
bed
may you be blessed!

Un Beso Is Not a Kiss

un beso
es una puerta
que se abre
un secreto
compartido
un misterio
con alas

un beso
no admite
testigos
un beso can't
be captured
traded
or sated

un beso
is not just
a kiss
un beso is
more dangerous
sometimes
even fatal

Poems

Andrea Teresa Arenas

Curve Ball

This vato   primes,
            turns tricks,
            delivers slick orations
all
            for La Raza.

This vato   struts,
            sways,
            juggles   the books
            and the lives   of people
all
            para La Raza.

He slips her between
rumpled sheets
to mount her   missionary-style
todo
            para La Raza.

Nikki

With a pushstart she
rises at 5 a.m.

off to the sitter by 7
into La Clínica near 8.

Putting anxious faces at ease
with her whisper-spanish
she cradles sick babies of los mojados,
comforts battered mujeres,
strokes the gray of aching
abuelos.

Locking up at 6 p.m.,
no throngs cheer her.
Her tributes come in
        nods of respect,
pan dulce y discos de Julio Iglesias.

"In Tejas I lived caring for ten,
so yo no tengo tiempo
para escuela.

Cuando yo came to Milwaukee I learned
inglés,
got my GED.
Pero, ahora I want to learn more.
I want to go to college.

I want to be SOMEBODY."

Cloaked in humility, she does not recognize
she is the one to teach.

CHANGE OF MENU

Life with WonderBread
began to taste like bleached sawdust.
After wandering white labyrinths
I search for essence amongst La Gente.

¿Entonces qué?
Entonces "él" entró.
Un amigo   at a price.
He's the new wave   combination plate of
Skinner with vato saavy
con ojos negros
that rip me   apart.

Shredding me thru his fingers
he slides onward
never breaking his stride
as the slivers that were   once me
mingled with those
who   passed before.

HOUSE CALLS ON 15TH STREET

Leaving the crowded bar,
cruising home
he pivots midstream   to continue   his search

Waking her from restless sleep
he rings her doorbell,
gaunt,
tired,
with lipgloss smudges on his collar
he asks to share her bed.

Too afraid to say no
she opens her door   to this man of multiplicities.

His satin tie drops to the floor
and with it   falls his bravado.
Shirt thrown across the dresser
and with it   lies his arrogance.
Slacks and underwear dangle at the foot of her bed
and with them   rests his machismo

Briefly scanning his nakedness in the mirror
he begins to rattle off the day's events.
Broken glass disclosures
sputter from his   brown   velvet   lips.

After sweaty adventures under the weight of comforters
he folds into a fetal cocoon
and asks   to be held.

Dozing off into dreamless sleep
neither one admits
lonely people   do not make love,
they only wrestle the shadows of sex.

THREE GENERATIONS

I

In a scant two hours
I knew her.

Zipping and zapping through her life,
I learned
        where she's been,
        how she got there,
        how she got out.

"I'm one of five," she said between
drags of her Carlton menthols
and sips of her fourth margarita.

"One of five, born to migrants . . .
only one to attend high school,
        much less college.

Law school was a bitch
(excuse my sexist terminology, Momma).
Professors make a hobby of picking the gray matter of students and
spitting the scraps out between their yellow teeth.
Pity the pobrecita
who didn't know her stuff.

I hated it up here when I first started grad school,
told my husband I wanted to drop out . . .

Couldn't tell the students apart . . .
they all looked *white* to me . . .
called all the guys Tim or Terry or Jimmy . . .

N'ombre, I called this poor chinga 'Shooter' for two years before
he had the courage to tell me his name was Gunner.

I dropped 30 pounds by my second year.

My last year
my husband would wake me from my
'screaming sleep.' . . ."

II

Did you ever pick?
Spent 16 years pickin . . .
I remember the rashes from the field and
polishing a freshly pesticide-sprayed tomato on my blusa
before crunching into it.

Who cares about tar and nicotine
Mira, I'm walkin DDT.

My ma
she's a trip.
When I got pregnant at 16 she didn't kick me out,
she asked me if Héctor and I had decided which college we were
going to . . .

She calls me every week.

Do you believe it,
no money,
but she calls every Friday to
cry   long distance.
"M'ija, I'm so proud of you, just think,
a lawyer. . . ."

All of Tejas knew when I graduated from law school.
Momma said there was one big fiesta in the Valley.

That woman lives on $3,000 a year
and she thinks I'm the genius . . ."

III

I took my daughter to the camps for a month
so she could see how the majority of us live.

I thought after ten years,
things would have changed.
Oh yeah, the camp 'houses' have refrigerators now,
no electricity,
but refrigerators.

My daughter picked some,
but spent most of her time
fanning the flies away from newborns in wooden crates
while their mothers and I stooped over strawberries.

At night we lay and
cried together.

My kid is tough
and sharp, ¿sabes?
When she was six she was upset because she couldn't decide if
                                                           she'd be
an attorney like Mom
or a dean like Dad,
so she decided to be the dean of the law school.

Now that I've passed my bar exam,
I'm anxious to get started.

Situations have to change, ¿ves?

There's so much work to be done
and there's no reason gente should have to live
with 'screaming sleep.'

Poems

Rosalinda Hernández

READIN' IS CHEAP

Readin' is cheap
Mama used to say
when speaking of her youth
Aside from beans y tortillas
and flour-sack dresses
it was the only thing
in this world
que tus abuelos could afford
for a familia of nine
then the simmering aroma
of chile verde
would choke her to silence
and with a final
piercing sigh
of contemplation
her lips would quietly plead
So why then can't I read?

APÁ

Calloused hands and sun-chapped skin
in the fields of ripened harvest
awakening the dawn
returning not 'till the sun came down
The aroma of tossed-up dirt
fertile soil on your boots
a familiar scent of labor
though fatigued and dismayed
the battle remained within

    "Go to school m'ija," you'd say
    "I work hard for you could be
    all I was not able
    learn to use your head and not your back
    like me
    who could only fight this battle with stones"

Then speaking of the hunger
the death of the twins
A story well recorded in my mind
of your many past seasons of tears
with a father lost in the bars
a brother behind them
a man at twelve with a struggle ahead
wearing shoes too big
too small
with six sisters under your years
a lonely walk in a boisterous wind

    "Go to school m'ija,
    learn to use your head and not your back
    like me
    who could only fight this battle with stones"

A lacerated heart
open wounds which never healed
a well-petrified man through your time
hardened and cold
A storm of bitterness escaping your breath
as you relived the days
when the world gave you its back
"Sorry Meskin, there's no job for you here"
A sting eternally felt
Charcoaled eyes
the inferno of your fury
now smoldered with helplessness

    "Go to school m'ija"
    now more a plea than a demand
    "Learn to use your head and not your back
    like me
    who fought all my days with a handful of stones"

Still grieving past seasons
of picking and plowing
from state to shack
shack to state
a temporary existence
of a migrant of time
reaping the harvest
of a lifeblood of famine
plagued by shadow
a darkness you could not escape
owning nothing but the clothes in a sack
and a pocketful of stones
to fight back with
It is your life Apá
a story told by a pauper's silent shout

A shout that grew to be my own
yet here I am today
learning to use my head and not my back
but like you
only able to fight this battle with stones

Landscapes

Juan Delgado

FOREVER THE NIGHT

The light of heaven begins
slowly to leave the landscape:
curtains of sky decline
to the sea's horizon;
on the waves that move
towards the white shore,
the sky fades into night,
and blue whales rest,
small mountains of sleep.
The circling birds fly away,
and from the East the moon rises
through the small mountains,
which have closed their eyes.

OFELIA

I couldn't fall asleep. Father again
was hungry as he came downstairs,
as if he carried something heavy
in his hands. Even in sleep it remained.
The doorways emptied, the rooms
began to change their light,
and as I stared into the window
my eyes met the eyes of my father.
We sat down together
to eat the last of the cabbages.
Both suddenly full, we nodded
to each other; he lifted me up
and carried me back to my room
where we found our beds, still waiting
for Ofelia to step out from the dark.

JALISCO

The train's heart pushes on
through the evening mist,
and its hum has slowly
put everyone to sleep.
From the seat of my compartment
the windows have the green
mountains of Guadalajara
moving in one dark shadow,
an endless horizon of night.
How long has it been, Jalisco?
Can I still begin again
to remember the face and body
that would have kissed me,
and put its hand on my shoulder,
whispering in my ear
about a morning in summer
when we had awakened together
near your open window.

WOMAN BEHIND A WINDOW

On the table next to you
your slender fingers tap
as your eyes take in
what has no color or shape
and carefully build a world out of all
the faint sounds of your imagination.
From the window the horizon ends
and the red necklace
around your skin catches light
while the landscape changes.
Tonight I will wait for you
to brush against my ear
with the news of the day.

ARRIVAL

The yellow cabs wait
by the Greyhound station.
One of the drivers
leans back to get light
from a street lamp,
so he can read a paperback
on the Second Coming.
He takes a deep breath
with his eyes closed.
It's late, much too late.
Further down the street
on a busy intersection
the women of Mt. Vernon
pass by in their fine dresses.
They dance their hips
as they walk away.
Some stay near a wall and wait
to tap on the shoulder, some wave
a hand in the air and whistle.

THE PHONE BOOTH AT THE CORNER

Grandfather took a walk
down to the neighborhood bar.
That day mother had placed me
under his care—
at sixty he was visiting us
for the first time.

We stopped near a phone booth.
Outside the bar in a cage
a parrot whistled back at us.

The phone began to ring.
Grandfather pushed the door,
forgetting he spoke only Spanish.
He raised the phone to his ear:
there was nothing he could do.

Again, he pushed the door.
He didn't understand
it was divided by hinges
and would only open by pulling in.
He pushed even harder—I could see
the fear in his face grow with his effort.

We were both unable to speak
as we pushed for what seemed minutes.
He finally stopped—exhausted
and the door opened.

He stepped out laughing.
I began to laugh with him
and the bird whistled.
All three of us
broke the air with our voices.

Poems

Víctor Avila

FOR THIS DAY ON WHICH I SAW
VALLEJO CRYING ON A STONE

With the hopes of a condemned prisoner
I look into the shrouded sky
and curse this May day
which falls around me like a mourner's shawl.

The phone is dead
and as silent as a badger lying battered
at the side of the road.

There is an anger inside of me
which one tear will not wash away.
I know an anger which one violent fall
down a flight of stairs will not distract from.

For this day has compounded itself inside of me
and I double over emotionally sick
as if a policeman had given me a rap to the knees.

For this day on which I saw Vallejo
crying on a stone I want to forever embrace you
with arms that are like firm vines entwined on a trellis.
And if this world is to beat us down with blows
then let us die in a chalice of God's tears
that on being brought to His lips
we shall experience our rebirth.

THE ROMANTIC NOTION

"mi corazón, te quiero infinito"

Around my wrist a red bandana
bought in '66 with Bolivian coins.
Then your memory was a soft vein of ore
that I would mine and soon rejoice in
as cigarette smoke filled still another cantina.

It's now 1967.
Ahead of me lie oil fields and insurrection.
I wait in a train station in Angola.
It's an oven full of flies.

When all fails here
I'll write you from Mozambique
where the gibberish in Portuguese
is unfamiliar to both of us.

I've waited for your letters
near every airfield and in every dusty village
where the machetes that once cut the sugar cane
are now raised against automatic rifles.

I once cradled inside of me
notions of a romantic nature—
            "I will die in a smokey trench
            looking out toward the Río Tama
            for then maybe, just maybe . . ."

After two years of contaminated water,
dysentery, and stolen rifles,
I have seen through my own field glasses
that we fight battles that aren't
worthy of our weapons.

There is a pier we once walked on.
With paper arms I reached for stars
that were violently unreachable.
You were a wonderful addiction
and your girlish kiss naive.

I no longer want to die drunk
but return home instead with Lorca's poems
stuffed inside my passport.

I want to plant a silver bayonet
underneath your feet
and talk to you for hours and days
of how I never missed you.

There's a DC-10 now landing in Los Angeles.
On it there is someone asking,
        "Did we have Paris?"
Yes, we had Paris.
And, aren't we both still magnificently alive?

Variations Between Worlds (Selection)

David Nava Monreal

CONVERSATIONS

Zona Rosa
      parasols
      cafés
little girls with brown skin
a maricón eating oysters by himself.

pass the butter honey
          shall we order another drink?
such a nice man to sell us a map of Mexico
          are the museums open?
the ruins are lovely this time of day
yesterday we saw an old couple riding a taxi
their lonely faces pressed to the window.
          they were heading to
Cuernavaca
    then Taxco
they were in search of silver
          did I tell you they weren't
in love, just living together.
          at their age?

Women prancing by in ornate clothes
      some Americans
      others Germans
      the maricón looks upset because he's
      lonely.

The French eat like pigs
> *did I tell you that Mexico*
> *City*
> *well, the Zona Rosa*
> *reminds me of Paris?*

when were you there?
never
but I read a book
the Eiffel Tower
Arc de Triomphe
Notre Dame Cathedral
> *pay the man*
they tip big in this section of the city
> *honey, the little girl*
stole the tip!
maybe she had a good reason.
> *the ruins are next.*

CONFESSION

have mercy on this Pocho
I'm sifting through the earth in search
of roots
don't laugh at my massacred
Spanish
(caló pidgin)
I know I stumble with every phrase
but I'm a second-generation
Mex-American
and I relate more to money and surf and blonde
ladies
than I do to open-air vendors.
Forgive me, señor, if I think the chile is
too hot

I'm a poor imitation
but at least I'm trying
and by the way
I like your silk shirt and yesterday
while wandering the museums
I swooned over a Diego Rivera mural.

I know, I know how pathetic I look
but I'm more American than
I think,
dig?

MIDDLE AGE

I no longer speak of poetry and music.
Are my eyes faded with dross and sin?
My hat is sitting absurdly on my head.
Maybe the pond has gone dry?

Can old coral be lovely again?
I saw it once on the Mediterranean.
Gaggles of girls in laughter and red.
Maybe the swans have fled?

Slide closer to me on this bench.
Isn't the marble stone cool?
Look over the trees and kiss me.
Isn't love in the park free?

I told you how young-looking you are?
Like early morning dew-drenched sky.
Am I laughing and telling you stories?
I must, I must learn to love love again

Purity

Wasn't it delightful that we
could behave like lovers the
first time we met? That we could
disrobe, unashamed, perhaps
brazenly, in front of each other.
That we could touch and examine
fetishly our quirks, dimples, and
moles and we could laugh away the
afternoon under the intoxicating
ambrosia of wine. Wasn't it
delightful that we didn't care
who we were but that we were humans
and we needed love and that is all
we sought? Wasn't it fresh that
the stars in our eyes were our
only identities? Wasn't it good
to create a sweet memory in the
present? Wasn't it fine just to be
alive and loving?

ON THE STRIP

City girl,
glitter,
dance among the lights,
ooze
Latin soul
like a ripe mango.
Show them what we
mean by
chula,
bonita,
in these summer nights
made sad
by old neons.
Bala,
history is dangling at
your sequined
skirt and love is
painted
on your
lips.
City girl,
you are my favorite sight
among the bobbing
tandos
and the half-smoked
cigarros.

CHURCHES

what are these grandiose rooms
                              these opulent altars of
gilded gold?
              why is there such a thick holy
silence between the pews?
              i hear novenas being counted out
in whispering voices.
              the priest murmurs and
his words resound against the marble walls.

a history lingers here among the murals
              the sculptured stations
candelabra collecting wax
              those crucifixes of nailed Jesus
staring, scrutinizing my soul.

i want out, into the bright Mexican sunlight
              i am not used to solemnity
there is death, otherworldliness
              inside the ancient edifices.

walls are cracked with age.
                    i seek youth, joy,
                              laughter
i cannot worship in sincerity
                    only in selfishness.

SUMMER

a summer evening
resounds with mariachi

> time to glance
> at the raven-haired señoritas

maybe a Dos Equis or three
and some impassioned conversation

> then I'll come alive
> like a Latin repressing his ancestry

peer into my coffee-colored eyes
and watch my soul

> coil, twist, then
> strike out like a viper

I'm alive in the summer nights
smeared thick with my culture

> the stars and moon
> awaken my personality

SOME WOMEN GROW COLD

Some women grow cold and retreat into
themselves.
They become almost impossible to
find.
You want to hear them laugh again
like they once did.
You want to touch them and watch them
unfold like a
morning flower.
But they're pained and they
carry that pain
around
like a great
numbing anesthesia.
And when night falls and
their men want to
make love to them
again,
the men have to become boys.
They have to learn
to make love
again,
from the very start.
They have to learn to be
tender, almost like angels.
They have to be innocent
and honest,
or their women will
never open up
like flowers any more.

Shadows on Ebbing Water

Lucha Corpi

2 October

The waters of the lake are still now. This morning, they curled under the gentle touch of the wind. Tonight, they rest. My heart beats faintly like an old timepiece whose mechanism has exhausted all miracles; and yet, deep inside me, another heart answers to the slow pulsing of my blood. I prayed for a child so many years. Why now? How can I leave Laz? How do I tell him? Where would I go?

I am tired of waiting for answers. I have waited too long already. There is no rest . . . Silvia, my cousin, my friend . . . She is no longer here and I have no one to confide in. I sit at this table every night writing, rewriting this story to have it somehow make sense. Laz has the answers, but he won't tell me. He and I hardly speak now. I know Silvia is in his mind as she is in mine, though neither of us ever pronounces her name. For the past few months, silence has been our accomplice and our own worst enemy, too.

Before you are born, my little one, before you are born I will find the answers. I owe you that.

. . . Moon shines cruel relentless cold the waters cold wish were ninety old not remember yesterday only long ago toy got for my birthday five years old sun shining mother smiling sixteen texas father proud cotton pickers don't want stooping rest of my life father you must don't get any ideas honest labor have to help don't want to be like you old drunk no ambition please antonio don't don't hit him hijo say you're sorry please i am not i am not beats you up leave him i will kill him one day don't say that no no go away live for both of us both of us never saw her again died because of him better not see him again must be something better out there beyond fields damned i don't want to remember eva you want to remember it all sit by the window writing looking for answers the truth i wanted to spare you damned wish didn't remember darian silvia lie with you there made smooth and clean by the

waters like a rock forget   forget   forgotten   left alone   all sins
forgiven no need for truth   no confessions   will won't   let go   eva
when will you smile again   don't you see   silvia is dead   let her
rest   accept her gift to us   accept . . .

30 October

There was a time when everything worked well. I met Laz when I
was ready for him. And he was also ready for me, he said. We were
happy for a long time . . .When Silvia's letter came announcing her
arrival after a fifteen-year-long absence, I was overjoyed. Silvia had
been more than my cousin; she had been like the mother I had never
had.

When she left Encinal, she was twenty-two, slender and full of life,
with luminous eyes like an autumn day just before dusk. Everyone
liked her, then; everyone looked at her.

The day she arrived back in town, hardly anyone noticed her. She
was very thin and seemed exhausted as she bent forward to put her
suitcases down beside her. She looked sad, but she smiled when she
saw me and, for a moment, her eyes regained their former brilliance.
We approached smiling, and holding back the embrace, we stood
before each other until our smiles became tears. She walked closer and
kissed me on both cheeks and softly wiped my tears and hers.

Many memories raced hurriedly through my mind. The morning I
fell down and tore my beautiful First-Communion dress on the way to
church. That other afternoon I cried because my menstrual flow had
come for a second time. No one had explained it would happen every
month for many years to come. The first time a boy kissed me and I
thought he had made me pregnant. Silvia was there to comfort me, to
explain and make it all right again. How I had missed her all those
years. But she was back, if only for a short time, and the rest didn't
matter.

"How long will you stay?" I asked her on the way to the ranch.

"I've come home . . . I don't know for how long . . . Perhaps forever . . ." Her voice quivered as she answered me; but I was so
happy to hear her say that, I brushed aside the ominous signs in her
voice. She recovered quickly and asked, "Tell me about Laz. What is
he like?"

"Handsome . . . Well, for me he is, has a great sense of humor,
knows a lot about a lot of things, never an unkind word, reads

everything he can get his hands on, always helping someone or this or that cause. You'll like him, I'm sure."

"Do you love him very much?" She asked almost in a whisper and answered her question immediately after, "Of course you do, I can see it in the way you speak about him. How lucky you are . . ." And her voice trembled again, and that time I could not dismiss it easily. I looked at her, but she didn't look at me. She leaned forward and looked out at the grazing lands, oblivious to everything.

It was then I realized for the first time how wanting of love Silvia had always been. There was much life in her, such love and generosity, and yet her eyes at moments like that showed a great dissatisfaction.

How little did I know of her? Had there been any men in her life? Was she coming home because of some romantic misfortune? Was she ill or going mad from loneliness? I did not dare ask her then, but in time, I thought, she would tell me.

. . . A pair of eyes looking at me from the darkness   eva it wasn't wrong   silvia and i   the dark side of myself   i of hers   understanding between us   like between old enemies old friends   no need to expose secrets   no loss   no rejection silvia and i   know   search find   never enough   more   better   higher   hoping   next place someone   the next one   causes   fools silvia and i   this passion ends   only   with   death   a grave   of water   dark   light   water time . . .

1 November

She wrote me many times during those fifteen years. Her letters were always full of details about school, work, later her business. She had gone to school against Grandma's best judgment. "Schools give you the wrong idea about life," Grandma would tell us both. "That'll just make you unhappy women. No man will want to marry you." But Grandma had made a promise to our fathers on their deathbed, on that horrible day the 205 derailed off Encinal and Silvia and I lost our parents.

Silvia never gave up her dream of a career. She convinced Grandma, and on a Sunday afternoon she went off to the city to work for Mr. Cassiano, an old friend of Grandma. She worked days and attended night school. With Mr. Cassiano's help, in time she opened a small dressmaking shop. In a few years, she was into fashion design. She began to travel on business then. She scarcely wrote me during her trips, but two weeks after her return, I would receive a present she had bought for me.

Up to the time I saw her again, I had pictured her life as a constant glamorous adventure in faraway places. But watching her on the day of her arrival I realized her life had not been an easy one. Yet, she had a dream and she followed it. That was Silvia, my beautiful cousin, my very unhappy friend. Maybe Grandma was right; maybe Silvia had had to give up the love of a man and a family to follow her dream. A dream ... At what price? I remember how outraged I felt that day. Silvia was bringing home to me the picture of an unfair world, out there, a world I had never seen or imagined existed. Why couldn't she have had both? Was it just because she was a woman? I tried to dismiss those thoughts. I did not want anything to cloud my happiness, but somewhere in me a need to find the answers was beginning to take form.

... No light now   water and darkness   eva in the beginning there was no light only water   endless   no abyss   no height   tide and forever   no misery   no sins   eva   eva there is no truth eva   no truth   only life   life   and   death now   death   darian mentor   true father   sun on our backs   shadows on ebbing water   ebbing water   the hydraulic power of the wind   boat riding the crests   running guns off the coast   caught   darian jump   no get away darian   i am here   go on   i follow   crabs everywhere rocks and crabs   sun   empty beach   was old   couldn't swim . . .

2 November

This morning I stood before their graves. Grandma and Silvia buried beneath my feet. I sat there for a while. It was peaceful and warm. I was ready to get up when I felt a short trembling just below my navel. It was like the soft flapping of wings inside me. Blood rushed to my face and my heart pounded in my chest as if to welcome the sign. And yet, I felt alone. All the people I wanted to share that moment with were unable to reach out and put their hands on my belly and touch you through me, my little one. The years of loneliness I had always managed to shun fell on me suddenly. And for the first time, I felt out of place in my natural surroundings. I did not belong any longer. But where did I belong? Mexico, I thought; I could go to Mexico, visit Grandma's hometown and all the other towns Grandma used to tell me about when I was little. Maybe I belonged there, but I knew I didn't. Mexico was my past, the place that smelled like my grandmother's clothes, a smell of fresh herbs, the smell of wet soil after the storm . . . a refuge.

On my way back from the cemetery, I went past the spot where Silvia and I walked on that afternoon she arrived. Then we had talked all through her unpacking and bathing. And after preparing a light supper we had sat in the back patio overlooking the lake to wait for Laz.

"I had forgotten how beautiful the lake is," Silvia said with a sigh.

"Yes, it is, but you must have seen many beautiful cities and lakes . . ." A silly comment I immediately regretted saying. I didn't want to awaken memories in her and make her long for any other time but then.

"Not as beautiful as this one now," she said and looked at me as if she could read my mind and wanted to put it at ease. "What made Laz want to settle here? He's from Texas, isn't he?"

"Isn't that reason enough?" I answered quickly and we both laughed. Grandma had always told us how ugly Texas was compared to California and how she hated those rude rednecks who had no love for the land, or for Mexicans, for that matter.

"Grandpa Lewis was the exception, of course," Silvia said amusedly, then looked away. "How wrong Grandma was. In the cities of California there is no love for the land or for Mexicans, either." She was silent for a while, then asked, "How did you convince Grandma to let you marry Laz?"

"Oh, that was no problem. Laz won her over. He told her he was the exception, too, just like Grandpa. And besides, his family had come from Mexico, too. Anyway, she was getting old and wanted to see me well cared for before she died."

"Does he come from a rich family in Texas? I mean . . ." Silvia hesitated, "You've never said anything about his family in your letters. . ." I knew she felt uncomfortable.

"Don't be embarrassed; I've asked him the same thing, but he doesn't tell me. He just laughs and says it doesn't matter," I answered in a low voice. I knew Laz was in the house. I could hear the water running, doors opening and closing discreetly, and his moving about getting dressed. "I guess I don't know much about his life before I met him."

"Has he ever taken you back to Texas to meet them?" Silvia was intrigued.

"No. He says his parents are dead and he doesn't want to see his brother again. He left home when he was very young and hasn't been back since. He enlisted in the army and was sent overseas. From there on I don't know much. He says he doesn't want to remember. He only wants what he has today, now, our life together on the ranch." I must have looked troubled because Silvia came over and put her arms around me.

"Maybe he's right. It's not important." She smiled. I tried to find comfort in her words and her warmth, but I couldn't.

"Anyway," I said childishly, trying to cover up my uneasiness, "it's all very romantic, don't you think? I'm married to a man with a *dark past!*"

Silvia smiled. She walked to the far end of the patio to see the sun setting on the other side of the lake. I stayed close to the door waiting for Laz.

He came out a while later and kissed me. We didn't say a word. I looked at him, gentle, always smiling as if he had no care in the world, and my doubts were dispelled.

. . . Cheated my way out of death always darian loved me like a son no idealist went along with me no children only me laz money is for you accept it can't accept it darian take it give it to the poor what you please don't care anything happens you are set for life bloody money darian can't refuse it laz blood on my soul not yours go they're near before it's too late i won't leave you darian such romantic go go they'll be here soon nothing left for you here boat on fire from the rocks single gunshot thundering in the inertness of the late afternoon from rock to rock to the small cavern darkness coldness stillness crouching a little boy numbness wanted to cry couldn't darian body growing colder colder crabs forced myself to eat vomited three times couldn't hold their raw meat darian nourishing me even after death eating his body through them tide finally took him back sea and time forever grave of water should have been mine crabs snapping off piece by piece while alive gunshots early morning noon late night men waging war to build peace naive like me worst kind of mercen-

aries we were pacts with the devil to win the way to heaven
something better beyond the sea beyond and i found you eva
and i found peace i thought silvia wasn't so lucky lucky
no she was she died and i live i live . . .

6 November

Laz stretches his legs, rubs them up and down, as if they
were numb. He is ready to get up and walk to the lakeshore as he
does every evening. He looks in my direction, but he doesn't
move from his chair. He seems to hesitate and then sags back in
the chair. I want to run to him, have him hug me, tell me
everything will be all right again. But I can't move from this
chair, either.

That first night Silvia spent here we stood together by the
door to the patio watching her. She seemed so enthralled by the
reflections of twilight on the lake waters, and was so still that,
for a moment, she looked like one of those beautiful manne-
quins I saw in a fashion magazine she'd sent me.

I was so eager to have them meet, I was ready to call her, but
Laz held me back. Instead, he walked toward her and stopped a
few steps from her. He looked intently at her. I stood motionless
by the door, and for an instant, I felt like a spectator watching a
play. I was the outsider. I saw them standing there, Laz holding
her hand, not saying anything. My imagination took off at full
speed. Laz had always teased me about my romantic flights. He
was right. As stupid as it was, I had already begun to see them as
characters in one of those syrupy, romantic novels I used to read
as a young woman. And I had forgotten they were my cousin
and my husband and not two estranged lovers meeting after a
long and painful absence. I was so caught up in their fictitious
love tale I had not noticed they were standing before me, looking bemusedly at me, Laz chuckling and Silvia waving her
hands in front of my eyes.

I came back from my reverie only to feel embarrassed, a child
caught in play-acting a torrid first kiss with a mirror. But I
laughed. I was always laughing then, at myself, at anything
that was funny.

Yes, it was a happy and fascinating evening that day my
cousin Silvia came home. Through all the trying and painful

evenings that followed after she was gone, I have chosen to remember that particular one. I listened to them talk about all the wonderful places they had visited. All of a sudden, Laz was transformed, renewed. He was fifty-one, but his face glowed youthfully. Before me was a man I had been married to for fifteen years, and a stranger at the same time, with whom I was falling in love all over again.

Yet in the back of my mind, questions were beginning to shape painfully and slowly. Why had he denied this part of himself to me? Why had he married me and settled here when he could have had an exciting life elsewhere? I couldn't even give him children. He was nineteen years older than I. Had I become his child-wife instead? God knows during our married life I had been as foolish and playful as a child; but he seemed to enjoy my foolishness, and I so wanted to please him it had never occurred to me someone in him starved for something else. But most of all, that night, I became aware of my limited experience. A sense of loss was beginning to seize me. It made me tremble.

I have never been able to hold pain, embarrassment, or fear for very long. So by the time I was preparing for bed, I had already dismissed those thoughts as quickly as they had come to mind.

... Silvia   the semidarkness of the patio   the desolate look at one moment   intense feverish brilliance in your eyes immediately after your lower lip trembling   flushed cheeks   dried mouth   quiet feeling of desperation just above your stomach   it was like looking into my own face   i wanted to put my arms around you   there is a way out   there is   instead i stood next to you   paralyzed   my own pain unbearable   it was all coming back   the man i was long ago   back to haunt me   you extended your hand to me   distantly   a cold hand trembling   i held it in both hands   we knew   silvia not brave like you   water   am so cold   moon shines   shines relentless   you mustn't lose hope   no hope laz   dying   few months   am so cold laz   i will hold you silvia   i won't go away   don't be afraid   not afraid laz   i don't regret anything in my life   pain   hurt   love   disappointment   hard work all my life looking for a place like this   no need to trade things off   explain them away   everything simple funny it had been here all along   laz i can't see you   am here won't go away   i want you to go away laz   i can't   you must

don't look back   we must spare eva   don't tell her   promise
laz   let her think kindly of me   she loves you silvia   she needs you
laz   go away   go back to the house   this i must do alone silvia
eva   silvia . . .

8 November

Deep beneath my skin, surrounded by my flesh, and nourished by
my blood you grow, my little one. You make your presence known to
me, though I cannot see your small hands forming or your heart
growing stronger by the second . . . If only I could tell Laz. I had dreamt
of that moment, I had wished for all the joy you would bring us. I'm so
happy you are here, yet so sad he cannot be with me, with you . . . I
sometimes think I cannot go away. I had no parents . . . Oh, Silvia.
Why did she go away? Why can't I know why? I can read the signs that
tell me winter is near or spring or autumn, but I can't know with the
same certainty why she left me, why Laz denies himself and her to me.

We were happy that month Silvia was with us. Maybe I was the
only one who was happy. She would grow pale sometimes, rub her
forehead. There were times her headaches were so bad she could
hardly open her eyes. I would make her lie down and draw the shades,
cook nourishing meals she would hardly touch. I would care for her
then as a loving daughter would care for a mother who worked too
hard. And like all daughters, I would shy away from the possibility she
would one day no longer be with me. I couldn't face up to her illness.
She was back with me and her presence was just as important in my
life as Laz was.

One night I had an awful dream. Laz was swimming in the lake
while Silvia and I watched from the shore. He would begin to go under
for some reason. Silvia and I swam toward him. We were midway from
where we had seen him disappear, when I saw Silvia struggling to keep
afloat. I was panic-stricken, unable to decide in which direction to
move, knowing I could only save one of them. Frantically I swam
toward the place I had last seen Laz. As I approached the spot, Laz's
body surfaced and his face turned toward me. He was dead, and Silvia
was nowhere to be found. I wanted to scream, but I couldn't. Instead I
kept slapping his face over and over with an anger I had not known in
myself until then.

The dream had been overpowering and the next morning I could
not get up. I felt guilty I had let Silvia drown, but most of all, I felt

ashamed I had punished Laz for dying too and blamed him for her death. And I wasn't sure at any given moment during the rest of the day whether I was more afraid of losing him or her. But I knew for certain, somehow, I would lose one of them.

That evening they both came in to keep me company. I broke down and told them my dream. They listened in silence. When I finished, Laz sat by my side and held me tightly for a long while, then left the room. Silvia stayed with me.

"I have an awful feeling," I told her. "You won't go away, will you?"

"I must, soon," she replied in a very natural tone of voice. There was no despair in her eyes. She was self-possessed and serene and beautiful, like a marble sculpture I had seen in an art book.

"I wish I could be like you, Silvia . . . go with you, travel the world over . . . I need to learn about so many things." I wanted to cry, but held back my tears.

"You know all you need to know to be happy, Eva. And you have Laz. He loves you and needs you. And I'll always love you too . . . Whatever may happen in your life in the future, remember we both love you . . ." And she smiled.

She stayed with me for a long time, and we talked. She wanted to talk about all the things we had done together when we lived with Grandma. And for the first time in my life I only listened, untiringly. Our years together, recounted by her, seemed different from the way I had perceived them before then. Oh, yes, I thought, I would join her soon and we would have many moments together while traveling somewhere. There was a great deal I wanted to learn through her, and after would come back to Laz a grown-up woman.

After she left, I fell asleep fantasizing about the many things she and I would do together.

Later that night, I was awakened suddenly. I thought I saw a shadow standing by the window. I looked for Laz in bed, but he was not there. I called his name, then Silvia's, but no one answered. I got out of bed and went to the window. The moon shone brilliantly on the calm surface of the lake.

I saw Silvia and Laz facing each other by the lakeshore. Silvia stood on tiptoes and kissed him, then ran into the lake fully clothed. I ran outside as fast as I could. From the patio I could see her swimming more and more slowly. I knew she was getting tired, but she kept on moving away from the shore. Laz stood on the shore motionless, watching her. She went under. I ran to him and begged him to swim after her; and when he wouldn't I tried to go after her myself, but he held me back. I didn't cry or scream, but I kept pounding on his chest with my fists until I fell to the ground exhausted. I looked at the lake searching, hoping. There was only a ripple left on the lake widening toward the oblivious shore.

I lay on the ground crying until Laz carried me back to the house. He kept muttering, "Better this way, better this way," and his tears fell on my face and mingled with mine. For days afterwards, I begged him to tell me, to explain, but he never uttered a word. After the burial, I moved into Silvia's room. Laz did nothing to stop me.

. . . Moon shining   relentlessly   night silvia died   eva how do i explain my cowardice   betrayed you silvia myself   took away her last few months of happiness   she couldn't betray you   i could   my life is a lie   a lie   can't tell you the truth   would you still stay with me   eva you are the real one   i am real only through you   i need you   stay with me save me   yes   take her away from here   yes sell the ranch nothing for us here   we must go eva   soon forget   forget . . .

10 November

Every night, I lie awake unable to dispel the image of Silvia sinking to the bottom of the lake. I call on every fantasy my mind can produce, to no avail.

It's been a long time since I had any pleasant dreams. Sometimes I miss my fantasies. Somehow they allowed me to get lost in a world where there was no pain and no questioning, but only pure delight. A time when the world had just been created and we were all new. Now I know that part of my life will not come again. I have nothing left but nostalgia and a thousand questions. Now I must learn to struggle, to seek out answers wherever they await me, fight for every bit of happiness I may have . . . Yours must not be the legacy of water, my little one. I can't promise you your father will be here with us. He must learn to fight for us, too. And perhaps, perhaps . . .

Grus Xicanus

Michael Ricardo

Late in the decade, the rocket cradling Juan Solís burst out of the valley in New Mexico, thus distinguishing the young man as the first Chicano in space. The newspapers predictably reported this fact in terms of equal opportunity and affirmative action. The current social historians no doubt will record the event as a watershed in the liberal program for the future. For Juan Solís, however, the flight signalled a critical development in the natural history of consciousness.

The flight occurred during the week walled between summer work and graduate study, early in September. The end of the nasty work of summer—spraying trees for blight and bugs—was a relief, but the prospect of another year of political science seminars did not excite me. The notion to witness the launch took easily. The trip would also afford a refreshing indulgence in my favored diversion, namely, bird watching, hitherto a secret interest so as to avoid the certain ridicule of my radical fellows at the university.

I told mother. Naturally she demurred, trying to imagine the reasons for such a silly adventure, but filled my request for a thermos of strong coffee. She beseeched me to stop and rest along the way. In the rearview mirror, I glimpsed her profuse benedictions at the doorway, blessings I mimicked by shifting gears as my truck pulled off the front lawn and away.

With seven days before the launch I drove leisurely towards the trans-Pecos of Texas, anticipating the start of the fall migrations. The road offered its usual array of carrion eaters, alleviated by the red flash of cardinals, the white-on-gray of the mockingbird, and the scatterings of verdins. The relatively mild heat of the day allowed for greater avian activity. I was pleased.

My plans included a stop at the town of Corbett, on the west bank of the Pecos River. Near the town, a recent excavation of the ruins of an Indian village produced fossil remains of large cranes, now extinct. The fossil find was doubly interesting in view of the sighting last year of several whooping cranes south of Corbett on the river's edge. The possibility of a new migration route in and out of Mexico intrigued me. Actually, in light of the fossils, it might mean the re-establishment of an old route for *Grus americana*, the whooping crane. It would be in the nature of a homecoming for the wasted whooper, a restaking of territory.

On the site, the lead paleontologist divulged details of the discovery, even permitting me to examine a few of the bone fragments. His attempts in the following days to place the finds in a broader context I found unimaginative. I began to build my own understanding. Contrahomecoming is the theme of history. Peoples leaping out of valleys, never returning. Visionless, unable to discern the roads homeward bound, like army ants forever on the march, we stumble upon others, other creatures, and displace them. As for the trumpeting crane, perhaps we are all their enemies, none innocent. The Indians, probably those who lived here long ago, hunted the fowl as game. There is an account of an incident wherein a crane pierced with an arrow thrust its vengeful beak into the breast of the hunter, killing him. Anglo stock enters the arena and crushes both. The migrations of Chicanos increase as the migrations of the cranes diminish. And I am perplexed by one writer's comment that, as knowledge of the species is grasped, danger to its range and habitat is foreshadowed.

I left Corbett for the Big Bend of the Río Grande suffering anxiety, with the fear that nothing happens, or that advances are at best made at a glacial pace.

The Big Bend was a furnace, and the birding is miserable "when all the birds are faint with the hot sun, and hide in cooling trees." I took refuge in a motel room near the park and read literature—a slim volume of short stories by the Argentine Borges and a book of poems. Between the icy sheets, I read and reread Keats's words: "The poetry of the earth is ceasing never." The image of the rocket came to mind: an earth-colored being inside a white ship, flying on blue flame. Can it be another of Earth's expressions?

On Friday, the day before the launch, the sun was less vehement. At mid-evening, when the land had cooled, I started for the Tularosa Valley, north of El Paso, in New Mexico. An excitement over the launch battled with the phantasms of night-driving. I marveled that the petty fears summoned by riding an unknown highway in darkness could compete with such a grand event for the attention of my mind.

Once in the valley, I pulled over to rest. Soon, first light dispersed the sprites of night, and the broad land and distant ranges gradually made their presence. I wondered why they chose this place. Surely the technicians fussed over the wind and sand, and the lack of a nearby ocean. The politicians must have prevailed. Turning off the main highway, I headed toward the hills which I guessed might afford a decent observatory.

Countdowns thrilled me, and I scrambled atop the cab of the truck, fixing my gaze through field glasses. The huge white rocket billowed smoke. The ground reverberated gently, not in defiance, but as if in cooperation. The ship rose in a slight spiral dance above the valley, the contrail dividing the blue uniformity. And the Earth flung the first Chicano into space.

Back to school. The radio program immediately regressed to pop music, offering an old Lennon lullaby. In El Paso, I lunched on menudo, tortillas, and cold beer. I took the reverie of the interstate. Perhaps in monotony I would pay less attention to the heat. The radio reported minor malfunctions aboard the rocketship; several coolers were failing, overheating the cockpit. I adjusted the vent on the left side of the dash, wishing the onrush of air to alleviate the perspiration between my back and the plastic seat cover. Thirsting for more cold beer, I drank several by the curb fronting an icehouse. Feeling empathy regarding the hot spaceworker, I poured a libation on the ground in his honor.

The sun set, and the first rest area invited me off the road. It was not far now to San Antonio, about one hundred and fifty miles. The beer consumed earlier was loosed on a tree stump in a thick, forceful stream. The relief brought sleep in its wake. Reclining, legs bent, on the bench seat of the truck I tried to sleep. The heat, humidity, and the mosquitos permitted only a light doze. At moments, between the insect deaths painted on the windshield, my eyes followed the moon-lit, erratic flights of bats feeding. I somehow knew that the bats waited to feed on the mosquitos which had fattened themselves with my blood. Sleep can be a devitalizing pastime, a possibility which annoyed me.

We met in November at the university in south Texas. The occasion was a symposium on the subject of ethnicity and technology.

It being one of the duties of a graduate student to ask a provocative question when the discussion founders, attendance was expected of me. Inexorably, the speeches wallowed in a lamentation over the bane of technological innovation on traditional ethnic cultures. Recalling what an anthropologist once said about the pick-up truck being very, very Navajo, I asked if rockets weren't very, very Chicano, in that Mr. Solís's mission was essentially migrant work on a glorified scale.

Mr. Solís smiled and said, "It was very hot up there too, but at least there were no flies."

Everyone laughed, and the jibberish continued about cultural inertia and the exponential dynamism of technology. The air conditioners servicing the auditorium galloped wildly though the November day was mild. Very Teutonic, I thought, shivering. Stealing away after several decorous minutes, I sought solace in a cup of hot coffee at the student center.

During the second tasteless cup, Juan Solís entered, circled by a squad of young brown men seeking counsel from the accomplished model, no doubt. They sat at the table nearest mine. I considered him. No longer the huge, white rocket, but a man. He was rather short, and fleshy even, wonderfully beyond the stereotype of the tall, lean astronaut. His skin hue resembled pecan shell, wet pecan shell. Dark brown eyes of course, and hair longer and more luxurious than mine. A moustache trimmed his lip. More Chicano than astronaut, I concluded. With a clanging of institutional chairs, the gang departed. Juan Solís joined me.

"Good afternoon, Mr. Solís," I said, rising.

"Call me Johnny. Did you enjoy the launch?" he asked as we shook hands.

"How did you know I saw the launch?" I retorted, puzzled.

"I would like to try and answer your first question, about just how Chicano rockets really are or can be."

We paused and got more coffee. He spoke.

"Up there, in la grulla blanca—that's what I call my ship, it beats the name, Reliant—I didn't sleep much. I didn't sleep at all actually, too hot; you read about the burned-out circuitry. It was hotter than those August days three years ago when even old mejicanos demanded twenty-four-hour library service to take advantage of the air conditioning. Usually, a hot afternoon will put a guy right out, but if it gets too hot, you might die, so your body stays awake."

My puzzlement increased at his reference to white cranes, as if he also knew of my secret avocation. He continued.

"I did get some sleep though. Every time I climbed into my space suit to work on repairing those satellites outside the ship, I'd fall asleep. I think I'm the first sleepwalker in space." We laughed and made a few lousy jokes about lazy Mexicans and siestas in space. But his story then took a mythopoeic turn, which I took in stride, for I began to feel like an accomplice.

"Like echoes, I caught dreams from far off, dreams that were my own. Though my dreaming them may be the echo, for I saw huge, white birds, like cranes—that's why I call my ship *la grulla blanca*—and I saw a nest, with an egg in it. And it was the egg that was dreaming the dreams that I have dreamed since I was young.

"There were three dreams in particular. One dream is about a young man praying, not in church but in a citrus orchard. He is praying sweetly, not in desperation or solicitation, rather in pure adoration. It's funny; he wears a tan cotton shirt with blue silk overalls. The young man also works on a ladder, but rather than picking oranges and lemons, he pulls them out of deep pockets and sticks them on the branches of the trees.

"Another dream stages a scene of umber-skinned girls, brighter colors in their eyes than around them. They're gaily eating watermelon in a garden, with prickly pear thriving in the shade of pomegranate trees. Their underwear, all of it, hangs drying on a chaotic web of rope, forming a canopy for the girls below.

"Yet in another dream—the one I love best—there is a giant pecan tree. Year after year, its brown fruit entices the brown fruit of the man and woman who reside nearby. The dream progresses. Each generation finds a different and creative, at times quite comic, method for harvesting the nuts. Twenty generations have passed peacefully under that tree."

We sat in silence for minutes. With sincerity I asked, "Are we descended from cranes?" I thought it was a compelling origin myth, with the migratory character our primary inheritance. *Grus xicanus*, a fine but tragic name.

"Who can say where we came from," he said, rubbing his temples with his thumbs. "I'd like to believe we came from the Earth."

I told Johnny about my trip to New Mexico, though he seemed to know much about it already, about the fossil finds near Corbett, and about the poem by Keats. And I related a speculative tale of my own, or rather, a tale from literature, the story by Borges which offered an antithetical vision. Called "Utopia of a Tired Man," the story concerned the chance meeting of two men in the plains of Texas, one a resident of the distant future and at least four centuries of age, the other a contemporary, common professor of literature. The future man informs the professor that space travel has been foresaken, such travel being no different than crossing a meadow to the neighboring farm. The professor also learns that men will come to choose the hour of their deaths and voluntarily hike to the crematory. Lastly, the future will also breed those who believe that "man is an organ of the godhead for universal consciousness."

"That's a fine story, and an honest one." Johnny's voice was distant, and his eyes vacant. "And maybe that will be the last chapter. But I think all dreams will come true. There are no shortcuts, and literature cannot serve as a shortcut; the Earth will not permit it. I can only tell you what I have experienced. Space travel is not like crossing a field. Years ago, I crossed many fields, only to find another with more onions beneath it. Too bad, with not only my feet in the ground but my hands too, yet so unlike a tree; more a migrant, like a seed always on the wind.

"There's no wind up there, en el cielo. It's quiet; I could see things, my dreams, or theirs, I don't know which. I could see backward and forward into the ages at the same time. I felt soothed; I'll get home, a home that is a gift from the Earth. Not something trumped up to cause trouble, not an invention to justify politics and violence.

"Those under the trees will die too, just like me. And their deaths will be mourned. The Earth has no use for immortality; gifts go unappreciated by immortals. And there will always be those who believe that men are godhead for consciousness. Our hearts reflect the ways of heaven, just as the Earth and the other planets reflect light."

Sitting alone, I realized Johnny had not answered my second question: how he knew of my trek to the New Mexican desert. Wondering about it infused my student life with a rare excitement. But I neglected my studies. Instead I wrote and published a tract on the end of migration, with cranes and all, and a splendid homecoming. It was a ridiculous utopia: no politics and violence, no worm-infested trees in need of spraying, and no Klansmen who dream of ridding the Chicano from the Americas. The derision from my fellow students was severe.

Before Easter, I withdrew from the university, actually suspended for nonattendance. I planned to visit Johnny. I never saw him again. On the way to mother's in San Antonio, the radio reported his death; he was killed by a drunk driver. How could I mourn him? How can one man, himself lost and now unhappy, mourn the extinction of a species, *Grus xicanus*, the latest exhibit in the museum of natural history?

Urbano: Letters of the Horseshoe Murder

Margarita Luna Robles

April 15

M'ijo—

I dont't believe this is happening. I've been so upset I can't eat or sleep. I don't know if I'll be able to go to work tomorrow. I don't even want to go outside of this house or even get out of bed. I can't face anyone. I can almost hear what everyone's going to say. Everyone always tells me you're up to no good, always in trouble, a real trouble-maker. Some of the younger kids' mothers say you're a bad example for their kids. Then they look at me. I'm the bad mother, it's my fault.

God knows I've tried. I've worked so hard! Why do you keep doing this to me? I work to support you, on top of always having your meals and clothes ready, and the house clean. I do it all for you! Maybe that's the problem—I do too much, I don't give you any responsibility. I do it so that you can study and be someone. I guess that's the end of your studies. You know how hard Tavo and I worked to get you into that school. They didn't want you 'cause of your record—now look!

This is bad all the way around. Mike's pissed off. I don't blame him. He's been more than a father to you, he's treated you right. Look how you pay him back.

Wait 'til your father hears about this. I haven't called him. Why should I be the one who always "gets it together"? Then no one appreciates it and I get blamed. Forget it. I quit. I can't take this anymore. I'm not going to talk to him. He doesn't care. He never took any responsibility for you after he left. I don't expect him to now. He's got three sons and a wife. He doesn't need the problems you make.

Randy, please tell me it wasn't you. I believe you. You're all I have. I have Mike too, but you're my baby. You and I have been through some times together. I can remember holding you so tightly while you slept, you were just a baby. I'd be so afraid of the dark I'd lie there crying, sometimes all night. Then I'd be afraid that I would die and there would be no one for you. I love you. I'm still here for you. I'm praying hard for you. *Be Good*—for me!

God be with you.

Love,

Mom

April 17

My Dearest Randy,

I love you. I'm so scared. The police came by asking me all sorts of questions. I didn't know what to say. All I said was I don't know anything and that we were at a party in San Francisco. I said that I don't know my way around in the City so I don't know where the party was at 'cause I didn't know anyone there. I was so scared I started to cry then my Dad got really pissed off and told them to leave and get in touch with our lawyer.

My parents are really upset about this. But it's not just this. They don't want me to see you anymore. They never have wanted me to see you. I wish they would leave us alone.

I get tired of all this shit.

To top it off your friends don't like you being with me. They always just ignore me, as if I'm not there. The girls don't even talk to me. They just stare at me, as if I don't belong there. I can understand that maybe they want to be with you, but it's not my fault that you want to be with me.

Randy, please tell me it's going to be alright and that you and I are going to be together. I love you too much to let you go. I don't want to be without you. I'll always be here for you.

Please write.

Yvette y Randy

PVM

April 18

Dear Randy,

How's it going, mi Locote? What can I say (?) except all shit's broke loose. The whole clica is acting like they got a stick up their ass. Everyone tries to be cool but they're scared. No one knows what happened. Three of our Homies got picked up for the shooting at the Studio 47. No one from the varrio was there and Yvette told me you guys were in San Fra at a borlo.

See, if you had been with me your face would've been seen and you'd never have got picked up. The only trouble you'd be in would be with Yvette. But you could really work that out easy, the way you always do. I know it's none of my business but why her? She's so out of reality. She could be fucking white for all I know. Whenever you bring her around it's like she's smelling CACA.

Maybe you lay that trip on her, not to mix or hang out 'cause the "loca" may rub off on her. And she's so clean, so untouched by the varrio, and that's what you want. If that's what you're doing that sucks 'cause I know and I have a good time when we're together. I know I make you feel good, cabrón. I also know it bugs you that I hang out with the vatos and I call it as I see it. The way I see it is I'm here. I'm waiting for you. Whenever you're ready.

I hope you get out soon. I miss your face.

Love,

Mousie—VHS

April 19

Randazzo,

I was glad to hear from you, homie. I guess by now it's getting to you, being locked up. Counting those fucking bricks gets real old too quick. The rap you've got keeps you away from the rest of the vatos in there. By the way, I knew Puppet got picked up for questioning but he's not out yet. This is a desmadre for the varrio 'cause la placa is playing "surveillance" in the Horseshoe. The vatos aren't even able to hang out at the park without the pigs busting in. We can't even walk the streets without being stopped. Last night one of the chava-leos got stopped and frisked: at gunpoint—the vatito is only 13!

Then they wonder why we don't got any respect. You know me, Ese, I've been around a long time, I've seen a lot. Que chinguen su madre, fucking putos. I could tell you alot of stories but they'll only censor them in the mail room there. I'll tell you when you're out. These are things you gotta know to survive 'cause now you got a chaqueta with la ley. So, you're gonna be getting it from la placa once you're back on the streets and, prepare yourself. You're also gonna get mierda from some of the homies. You gotta understand that the heat's on in the varrio, paranoia has hit everyone, and then there's the vatos who want rank over you. They're gonna use this in their favor. You know who they are but not everyone in the varrio knows.

The challenge is yours, Homes.

Después

OSO—VHS—SJ—14

April 19

Dearest Mom,

I got your letter. I guess you're pretty worried. I'm sorry. I know I keep blowing it. But, I didn't do it. You'll see. I'll be out of here in no time. They don't have anything on me, I'm just a suspect. There are no charges.

Never mind about what people say. I keep telling you that's a real problem you have, always worrying about what everyone will think and say. I hope you're feeling better and that you're going to work. This is nothing. I swear.

Tell Mike I'm sorry and I'm glad he's there for you. He's firme, even if he's not a vato loco and never was. He's been good to me, always let me be me.

Don't worry about el jefito. He's never around when I need him so he shouldn't say anything about anything. If he wants to help, fine, if he doesn't he should butt out. His sons aren't so bad—they are my half brothers, even if we never see each other or spend time together. Have you seen Stretch? He looks just like me, but bigger and I'm a vato loco and he's a jock. I like him. I always wanted a kid brother, I mean he is a kid brother but he's never around. You know what I mean.

Dad probably knows. the word gets out quick in the streets, Stretch knows. Don't bother calling him. Let him call you. Don't worry, O.K.? I'll be out soon. I miss your cooking.

I love you, Mom.

Your son,

Randy

April 20

Q-Vo Oso—

I got your letra, Homes. Good to hear from you. I swear I needed to hear from you. People write, you know what I mean? It's different with you and what you got to say. You know what I'm going through. I'm going fucking crazy in here.

I've been in here one whole week, I mean I've been in here longer than that before but not like this. I think they're playing games on me. I still don't got a court date, and there are no charges. They can't keep me here too much longer. You don't think someone is throwing a rata on me, do you? Or, maybe they think they can get someone to say I did it and it'll be pretty soon so that's why they won't let me out. The last time I broke probation and skipped the county line and fucked up by driving off the cliff in Santa Cruz. I guess that could have been worse, I could have killed myself. But it's illegal to keep me here like this, but they're still doing it. They said just the fact I broke probation again will keep me here. This fool told me I broke probation by going outside the county without a legal guardian. You know how I told you I was at a party in San Fra. My probation officer hasn't even come around.

I guess what's really bothering me is that it's Saturday night and I ain't getting any. Mousie wrote me. Boy, she's something else . . . I told you. She don't make it hard for me—ha ha, actually, she makes it very hard. She takes care of it, too. She's got huevos, she could have been a varo. She'll tell you off in no time. She's good to me, but I know she ain't fucking loose. She says she'll wait for me. What do you think?

Yvette wrote to me too. I love her. She is so nice and different than any of the other rucas. Except Mousie. I want Mousie in reserve. You know, when Yvette can't make it. But, oh boy, Yvette. She's soft, like a dream. She smells like warm milk, and she tastes so good. Everytime I kiss her, it's like I don't want to stop, like being lost in a cloud that floats, forever. Boy, I better stop. This only makes me think that I ain't got either one. Tonight I'll thank this fucking system for not tying my hands up.

Do me a favor, Homes. Get in touch with Father Mateo at the church and tell him I need to see him. I need to talk to someone soon. He's the only one they'll let in.

Drop me a line.

Your Homie,

Randazz-O

V_HS—San Jo—14

April 20

Randazz-o,

What's going down, Ese? Seems you're on a streak—puras chingaderas. Could it be you're getting a little too sloppy, not covering your tracks?

This is the third time you get picked up in one month—for different cargos. ¿Qué pasa, ése? The word out on the streets about this rap ain't too good. You're getting in over your head, vato. The first time was grand theft, the second was suspect in a case of arson, and now this.

You know what they say, Locote, the third time is a cinch. You're in: Big Time Felon. You're not even eighteen! I guess that gives you rank in the streets, in the varrio. Rank don't rank where you're at. I could have told the Homies about you—you're a bit too pushy too soon. Your timing is off and timing is what you need to be on top. You bring desmadres on yourself and you bring it on the rest of us. Varrio Horseshoe is hot with the pigs 'cause of you and nobody's liking it. Between you and me, Homes, I think you're better off in there.

Of course, this could be a game la ley is playing, trying to put a torcida on you for good. Lock you away. Being the leader that you are in the Horseshoe they want you off the streets.

But, I don't think so. Like I said, this is between you and me. When you get out, IF you get out, we'll take care of business. Just you and me. Suave.

Al Rato,

PaYaSo

San Jo Norte—14—VHS—Y—Qué

A DIALOGUE WITH NO ONE AT THE PARTY
IN THE HORSESHOE

4/20

FLACO: H-e-e-e-y, party time. Let's get down.

TINY: Alri-i-i-ght, look who's here, el Rocky.

CINDY: It's about time someone had a good party.

MELINDA: I know, it's been a rough week.

MOUSIE: You ain't shittin', I miss Randazzo.

ROCKY: Randazzo? Fuck. Three of our Homies are locked up.

TINO: Hey man, we ain't locked up. Cut loose.

LITTLE MARY: Don't be so cold, how would you like it?

ROCKY: Hey, man, you're getting too much foam in the beer. Pump it
   right.

J.R.: Beer? Who's got the goods?

LA SHORTY: What goods you talkin' about?

OSO: No la rieguen. You know the fuckin' pigs are out.

RICO: That's what I like: *order.*

LITTLE MAN: Hey, Mousie, you wanna dance?

PINO: With all these lovely ladies here, who wants to dance?

MANUEL: Change the fuckin' record.

BEAR: Yeah, put some oldies on.

EL RAY: Dim the lights, let's get close.

PAYASO: Hey, Mousie, I heard who you been fuckin' with.

MOUSIE: It ain't you, Puto.

LA SHORTY: Alright, Mousie.

LITTLE MARY: That'll show you.

CINDY: God, Mousie, you got a lot of nerve.

VERDUGO: Some rucas around here think they got huevos. They
   don't.

DREAMER: Leave the rucas alone. Let them have huevos for breakfast.

PAYASO: They can have mine right now.

OSO: Córtense el pedo con las rucas. Show some respeto. It's good for
   las rucas to be strong.

EL RAY: My, my, look who's here, la Rosie looking mighty fine.

ROSIE: Hey, Ray. Cyclone and Beto are out there waiting on some of
   the other guys.

PINO: Hey, Cyclone better not be packin' tonight.

CYCLONE: Someone say something about me packing?

BETO: If some of you ain't packing, that's your problem. Chisme has it that . . .

TINO: Yeah, we heard, Vickie's Town is coming down tonight.

OSO: Who's worried about Vickie's Town? I heard Lomas is after them so they ain't moving outside their turf.

LA SHORTY: Yeah, but I heard that Lomas got a pleito with us too.

VENADO: Things are hot in San Jo, O.K.? No varrio has it good with any other varrio. Pinchi Lomas always has a pedo with us. Every fuckin' time we get down, they run crying.

MANDO: Hey, man, this is a party.

OSO: Shut your fuckin' mouth.

CINDY: Who's pumping the keg? We're still getting too much foam.

EL RAY: I'm pumping . . . the keg, Cindy, the keg.

BETO: I'm feeling really fucked up.

CYCLONE: It was that shit you were smoking.

ALBERT: Who's got fuckin' shit to smoke?

OSO: You guys better cool it.

MOUSIE: You nervous, Oso? Have you heard from Randy?

MANUEL: Hey, the never-ready sisters are here. Get it, Navarette, ne-va ready?

LINDA: You can hear this party on the other block.

STELLA: Who's got the whites?

MIMI: Whatever you do, don't get redded out.

PINO: I got some dust.

ROCKY: Heddy and some of the other vatos from Little Town are here.

MIMI: I saw Chino and his brothers out there, too.

LINDA: That's alright, Little Town locos are fine.

MOUSIE: It's good that smaller clicas get it together with us.

MANUEL: Except for Varrio Libre.

OSO: Shut the fuck up.

ALBERT: This is a good party, people are dancing and singing and getting high shaking up the dust.

BETO: That dust was good, made me think of my mother.

TINO: That dust got around tonight.

EL RAY: You guys blow it with dust.

CINDY: You wanna dance, Ray, or are you waiting on Becky?

MOUSIE: Angel baby, my angel baby.

LITTLE MARY: OOO-HOO I love you, OOO-HOO I do.

MELINDA: No one could love you like I do.

LINDA: Alright, turn the music up.

OSO: We can't have the music louder or the pigs are gonna come down.

TINO: Or Vickie's Town.

ROCKY: I got my shank.

CYCLONE: I got my cuete.

PINO: I got my dust.

BETO: I got my ruca.

DREAMER: But did you bring your huevos?

OSO: Look, it's after twelve, maybe we should call it a night.

TINO: But there's still beer in the keg.

ALBERT: And there's still plenty of dust.

HEDDY: And there's still plenty of rucas here.

OSO: Is that all you guys think about? Drugs, cuetes, and rucas?

LITTLE MARY: Wow, there's about 50 people here tonight.

MOUSIE: There's cars parked for two blocks down.

LITTLE MAN: EVERYBODY STOP! TURN THE MUSIC DOWN! CUT THE LIGHTS!

CINDY: What's happening? I gotta go, I gotta go.

LA SHORTY: Shut up, Cindy, get down!

BLAST! BLAST! BLAST! BLAST! BLAST! BLAST! BLAST! BLAST!

MOUSIE: Little Mary's down!

MANUEL: Flaco's hit!

BETO: I told you guys, you better be packing.

OSO: Nobody panic! Just stay down on the floor. Girls, stop screaming! You're not doing anything for Little Mary by screaming. Mousie, get to the phone.

ALBERT: What's going on, Man? Is it the dust or is this for real? Oh, man, get me off of this shit, I don't want to die.

CINDY: My mom told me not to come.

EL RAY: My mom told me to stay home, come on, Cindy.

DREAMER: FUCKIN' VICKIE'S TOWN—THE WHOLE GANGA IS HERE! WHERE'S THE FUCKIN' PIGS WHEN YOU NEED 'EM?

OSO: THIS IS A SET-UP. FUCKIN' NARCS. THEY'LL LET US KILL EACH OTHER OFF FIRST! MOUSIE, DID YOU CALL THE FUCKIN' PIGS? STAY DOWN AND SHUT THE FUCK UP OR WE'RE ALL GOING DOWN!

MOUSIE: Little Mary's still breathing . . . Operator, this is an emergency. There's been a shooting, we need an ambulance. Two people are down, there's a war outside, there's shooting.

LINDA: My God, Flaco's not breathing. FLACO-O-O-O-O, FLACO-O-O-O-O!

CINDY: Oh, Flaco, please don't die.

CYCLONE: DON'T GO OUT THERE, BETO, BETO, BETO!

STELLA: BETO'S DOWN, BETO, BETO, BETO, BETO!

ROCKY: STELLA, GET DOWN!

OSO: FUCKIN' ROCKY, LET BETO BE. DON'T GO OUT THERE, BETO, DON'T GO!

MOUSIE: GET THE FUCKING POLICE OVER HERE RIGHT NOW. WE'RE ALL GONNA DIE. 3-3-0 SPENCER, NOW!

CYCLONE: EVERYONE QUIET! SHUT UP! WE GOTTA THINK! OSO, PINO, CHINO, RAY, LET'S GIVE IT TO THEM! VARRIO HORSESHOE RIFA Y QUE!

EL RAY: You ladies stay low, watch Little Mary. Let's see, Mousie, get a towel, and press here, like this, you got it? Cindy, leave Flaco alone. Linda, watch Cindy, get her calmed down.

CRASH! CRASH! CRASH! CRASH! CRASH! CRASH! CRASH!

CHINO: Oh, man . . . Look at my ranfla . . .

MOUSIE: Get away from the window, Chino, you're gonna get your brains blown out.

OSO: This is it, Homies. Get your cuetes, fileros, out the garage, get the tire irons and the axe. ¡Vamos a darles en la madre!

STELLA: The ambulance is here.

EL RAY: Here comes the police force . . . Oh, wow! I hope they don't blow our vatos away. Vickie's Town culeros just split.

OSO: TRUCHA! We ain't gettin' them here tonight.

DANNY: FUCK . . . Look at all the pinchis ranflas.

OSO: Look at my fuckin' house, man.

PINO: What the fuck brought this down?

HEDDY: Rocky and Beto are hit. . . . Rocky's doing real bad . . .

VENADO: Pinchi Tinto de Vickie's Town had a pleito with . . .

OSO: No, Officer, we don't know what happened, we were just having a party . . .

April 21

Dear Randy,

Just a few lines to see how you're doing. I hope you're O.K. Randy, I hate to be the one to tell you, but I have to. There was a party last night at Oso's. Some vatos came down from another varrio and blasted the house. They got Flaco—he didn't make it. We were all inside the house. It must have been about 1:30 in the morning. We were dancing, partying, just having a good time when it all came down. Flaco was right there, just there checking it all out, smiling like he always did. . . . He got hit right there. We tried to get everybody down but it was too late for Flaco. He got hit in the first round.

Nobody was supposed to know about that party for the same reason. You know how the Horseshoe is right now. We got pleitos going with every other varrio in San Jo, it seems. Everyone was inside—thank God. Otherwise they might have gotten more of us. Beto and Rocky got hit too. They went out to get into it. We don't know about Rocky. He's in critical condition. He got hit in the leg and there's a bullet right near his liver and they can't take it out. His sister told me that he might bleed to death if they try to take it out.

Beto had surgery. He got shot in the shoulder. He's going to be O.K. I wish you were out. It's sad around here. I wish Flaco was here. Why him? I really wish you were here to hold me. I know you'd understand, you know how close Flaco and I were and I know how close you were to him, too.

Now we got Rocky to worry about. And Flaco's funeral. His family is really torn apart. God, I can't stand this! Please write.

Later.

Love,

Mousie

April 22

Dear Mousie,

I'm so sorry about Flaco. I wish I was there to hold you. Damn it! It pisses me off. He was just chavaleo—he was firme. He never messed with anybody. He always ran from pleitos. But that was good! He knew he couldn't hang so he avoided it. The vatos used to get on him at first about it. But later it was like everyone respected him for it. 'Cause all of us knew it took more huevos to walk away from it. Then later it was like we all took care of him, sometimes we'd take him home before the chingadera started.

I just wish I had been there. I wish I could get out of here. It looks like I'm needed at home. I'm surprised Oso didn't see it coming. Oso should know better than to have a party when everything's hot. He knows the word always leaks out about parties.

Mousie, I know this is a hard thing for you. That's what life's about in the varrio, and you're a part of it. You gotta show your strength now, for Flaco's familia. And for Rocky too. Pray that he makes it. If he doesn't make it, that's just gonna make the payback a little tougher—and as it is, it's tough right now.

You know what, ésa? I miss you, too. I got a hearing tomorrow morning. So, say all your prayers and light all the candles you can and maybe I'll see you tomorrow nite.

Cross your fingers.

Al Rato,

RANDAZZ-O

April 22

Oso—

¡Qué desmadre, ése! Some vatos from Varrio Libre got picked up on Sunday and I got the word. Mousie wrote to me and told me about Flaco. Of all the vatos, man. That chavaleo had a lot going for him, a lot of corazón. He would've never hurt anyone. What a waste!

I'm getting tired of this. This year we already lost three homeboys because of the gangbanging. If Rocky doesn't make it . . . I don't even want to think about it. They were all firme, too. I just can't accept it about Flaco. Oh, man, his poor familia.

All this shit doesn't make it easier for me in here. I'm just trying to keep clean in here. I'm glad they're keeping me away from everyone in here. Horseshoe is in mierda with all of San Jo, it seems. Tell the vatos to stay clean—it's worse in here right now. You better start thinking about how some of this shit's gonna start straightening out. The varrio ain't in no position to do any paybacks—not even on Flaco's life, Ese. The killings have got to stop!

Tú también la regaste. Why did you have a borlo? This was the *worst* time. You know there's mierda going on with our own homies. Some of our own vatos are trying to take over. That always makes for snake movidas. I know they wouldn't pull something with another varrio, but still. Some mouths start flapping and it's over. Word gets out on what the varrio is doin' and everything backfires.

But listen, ése. I'm not trying to tell you what to do. I'm just letting off steam. Being cooped up in here is getting worse. Right now I could punch out the walls with my bare fists. I've been having to deal with the maddogging from vatos I consider to be just plain fuckin' putos. But, I want to stay clean. I gotta get out of here. Maybe I'll be out for Flaco's funeral. I got a hearing tomorrow morning. They don't got nothing on me. They gotta cut me loose.

If you don't see me tomorrow afternoon, write back to me. I hope you don't have to.

Después,

RANDAZZ-O   V$_H$S-Norte-14-y qué

April 23

Puppet—

Q-Vo, Homes. I finally got out. I had my hearing this morning and they had insufficient evidence to make any of the charges stick. So, I'm back on the streets.

The timing is right. I guess you heard about all the pedos out here. Flaco's funeral is tomorrow and the rosary is tonite.

Listen, ése, llévatela suave in there 'til your hearing. The Horseshoe has too many pleitos going, so don't trust no one. They gotta let you out. They busted you for questioning only. They're just running jueguitos on you. Just like me, they gotta turn you loose.

This one's a short one. I gotta get ready for the rosary and pick up Mousie. She's taking it really hard. Write to me.

Al Rato,

RANDAZZ-O

A PARADE

El desfile de luto. Cuerpos entristecidos marchan. Así. Se acercan. La banca al frente del altar. Un crucifijo con un mono de enplaste cuelga. Sobre la caja. Esa caja eterna donde en paz descanse. Los cuerpos siguen. En rueda. Por medio de las bancas caminan. Se hincan. Se agachan sobre la caja. Dejan símbolos: besos, retratos, medallas, lágrimas. Las lágrimas. El llanto de una madre. El hueco de la iglesia. El eco de los sollozos. Las lágrimas los llantos los sollozos no llenan lo profundo de este dolor. Los abrazos. Vacíos. Las flores. Tanta flor. Tanta gente. No hay conformidad: lo siento mucho . . . que Dios lo tenga en paz . . . aquí estoy . . . si necesita algo . . . le acompaño en su dolor . . . es lo que quiere Dios . . . así lo quiso Dios . . . ahora está en la gloria con Dios . . . ya no sufre su flaco . . . tanta pena estos jóvenes . . . estoy con usted en su dolor . . . estoy rezando por usted y su familia . . . su alma ya está libre . . . confórmese . . . ya no llore . . . llorando no lo deja descansar . . . le atrasa su viaje al cielo . . . hay que tener conformidad . . . hay que tener fe en Dios . . . El es el que nos da y nos quita . . . El sabe por qué . . . El sabe por qué hace lo que hace . . . tenemos que pagar nuestras deudas . . . tarde o temprano . . . mejor en esta vida que en la otra . . . él ya pagó . . . él ya descansa . . . ya no llore . . . tiene sus otros hijos . . . dele gracias a Dios por sus otros hijos . . . tiene que ser fuerte . . . usté se tiene que dar valor . . . Dios está contento . . . El ya tiene otro angelito . . . su flaco . . . un angelito . . . él todavía era un inocente . . . él no supo de los males de la vida . . . dele gracias a Dios . . . Dios no más se lleva lo bueno . . . lo inocente . . . siéntase orgullosa . . . fue escogida . . . Dios no se olvida de usted. El pobre hombre al lado de su mujer. Su hijo de él: también. Nadie más. Los dos sienten: su muerte.

Memoir: Checker-Piece

Juan Felipe Herrera

It took place in a tan two-story East L.A. Victorian. Somehow, the four of us were participants in an odd game in which all the players had to intersect at this particular cubelike dwelling.

It was a checker-piece in the center of a checkered infinity. All the houses seemed to be exactly alike, as if they had been pressed through a sharp grill in the stratosphere and softly and silently flattened into a two-tone grid in the hottest ground of Chicanoland.

Everything was patterned: veridian green lawns snipped with the grace of a ballerina, probing T.V. antennas plucking messages through the smog, and a score of plump off-white 1952 Plymouths; everything aglow beneath the perforated and hazy Plexiglas box in heaven.

Tomás Mendoza-Harrell had invited me to come over. I had met Tomás a year earlier, in 1970, at Royce Hall Quad at UCLA during the early planning stages of a raucous trip to Chiapas. He said he had a film project in mind for me.

He had gone through the usual Chicano male initiation rites held at Santa Colby, an Ozzie-and-Harriett, two-bedroom house in Santa Monica, which a brown horde converted into a hallucinating den of first-generation EOP undergrads drinking papaya tea and sangría, eating Quaaludes and tortillas, listening to Santana and Satie, talking about Quetzalcoatl and revolution as we planned the next raunchy Molotov attack on the Greek fraternities and as we ditched Juan Gómez-Quiñonez's Mexican-American History-B class.

He picked me up in his rebuilt Volkswagen bug, La Cucaracha.

At the time I was living in Venice trying to eke out an enlightened existence on EOP loans, macrobiotics, Crayolas, poetry, and a holistic relationship with Lynne Erlich, a Jewish-Russian-Mexican-Chicana poet who had just broken up with the lead singer of the 103rd Street Watts Band.

As usual, once in the belly of La Cucaracha, we became two phosphorescent rap machines unraveling new ideas for the sweltering lowlands of Aztlán.

Tomás's green eyes punctuated the plan: "Look ése, I want you to meet Gerandline Kudaka when we get to the house. She's gonna do camera while I direct. Anyway, it's a Neo-Mayan Chicano urban thing; we'll talk about details later."

I told him to roll down the window.

He had already been trying to teach me Ken-Po Karate and the heat was bloating my sore 130-pound brown rice-fed bod. It was an interesting film concept, I said, but at the moment La Cucaracha and its envelope of air overpowered me.

Everything was too real. It was as if we were traveling inside of a Magritte painting, careening through a freeway made of cotton spiraling into a labyrinth of neatly scissored origami residences.

La Cucaracha whips through the maze. Tomás's green lights go on again: "Watcha, you are wearing khaki pants, OK? No shoes, no shirt, me entiendes? You are walking through a tunnel with a hood over your face, but there is a way out; you are alone groping through a dark cosmos, you hear voices, moans, things are clawing at you, you are trapped in a damp chamber of voids, secretions, and suffering figures. What do you think?"

I realize that the rap we had a couple of weeks ago at Santa Colby on the Mayan concept of the Underworld, Xibalba, is about to go on screen.

"And then," he blurts readily, clutching the plastic donut he uses to steer the Cucaracha rocket, "we are going to tie you up on a boulder in a hiding place I know of in the Santa Monica Mountains; it's perfect for this scene."

"What about Geraldine?" I ask. The wiry Chicano space pilot quickly responds: "Never mind, once we get you tied up, I want you to start screaming, snarling, shaking your head violently, left and then right." "Uh huh," I mumble, gazing at the architectural precision of the eerie landscape we are approaching.

Tomás continues, crouching forward. He looks like he's about to ski into the windshield. "Remember Anthony Quinn in *The Hunchback of Notre Dame* and how he distorted his body?" he adds, on the verge of standing up and jamming his head through the roof.

"Simón, yeah, I know." I ponder through the glass.

"Well, that's how I want you to move your torso and upper body while La Geraldine whips you." He lifts his thin left eyebrow professorially as he elaborates: "You know, this is the most important part of the film."

"You ain't kidding, carnal. It sure don't sound like viva Humpty Dumpty," I quip and stare at him.

Tomás settles into his seat again. He appears to anticipate a negative vote on the film. I turn and look out the little window again. Everything looks so identical.

I think about contrast.

Last summer Tomás and I were walking through La Plaza Central in San Cristóbal de Las Casas after bribing a pilot to fly us to the Lacandon Jungle. I bought the day-old Excelsior paper from Mexico City. As I paged through it thinking of a shortcut to Comitán, the takeoff point to the jungle, an odd rectangle of letters slipped into my mouth. I whispered:

MUEREN VARIOS EN MANIFESTACION CHICANA.

Rubén Salazar is blown into careful confetti squares in the smokey web of the Silver Dollar Bar by the L.A.P.D. swat-pig.

I see a thousand stitches being sewn over the bleeding streets, tying up the swollen sidewalks like skin.

I think of Little John Angulo somewhere in Westwood writing his last metallic note on the jagged blue line of his left arm. And no one would hear his last poem of desire and no one would applaud his hard pride as he fixed his eyes on the dead wall forever.

La Selva Lacandona appears.

José Pepe Chan Bol paces the makeshift airstrip at Naja in the heart of the Lacandon Mayas. He has come to accept malaria in his village like a predictable storm. He has become accustomed to playing Christian Baptist preacher and reciting the Bible from Maryland in the thatched-roof temple that his sons built. The only thing that bothers José Pepe Chan Bol is the air.

It smells like a fuse burning.

He can hear the green time bomb ticking among the vines of the forest. Near Chancala, he can hear Joaquín Trujillo, one of the government's latino henchmen, drink post and stake out Lacandon land for timber, dolomite, and rubber. And not far from the airstrip, José Pepe Chan Bol can see where the fuse has scarred the earth, stripped the land, and left a road of stiffened patches for the next bulldozer from San Cristóbal.

But on the freeway of East Los, looking out of a luminous Aztlán space shuttle called La Cucaracha, no matter how hard I try, no matter how hard I attempt to focus, I see no contrast.

I think of Venice again.

I could be eating some fluffy brown rice with a touch of tahini sauce over a half-glass of water. I could be in my closet converted into an art studio sprinkling glitter on my latest Chicano Matisse crayon nudes. I could be brushing Lynne's thick black eyebrows as I prepare to do one of the special Chicano-Bogart lines like, "What's a chavala like you doing in a canton place like this?"

But I am here next to a kamikaze compadre zooming on a one-way mission to the gut of Aztlán as he unravels one of the aesthetic battle plans in the Chicano Movement's war against the Kapitalist dragon.

I crack open a bottle of warm spring water that I always carry in my handwoven bag, and take a swig.

"Check it out, carnal. Who's going to hear me scream and snarl à la Anthony Quinn under a dirty black burlap sack, humping on a rock in the middle of nowhere in a five-minute 8mm film done by some oddball from San Francisco regarding some kind of urbo-Mayan-Chicanoid chingadera that you came up with?"

I lean back. I look through the stained amber sunroof. La Cucaracha is on cruise control. Tomás peers at me with one eye as he scopes the freeway for the next off-ramp, humming one of those whimsical tunes you hum to paste desperate moments together. I lean over and whisper to the Aztlán pilot, "I love it, I love it."

We break out into our Cinco de Mayo special mariachi yell and rattle out some of the finer aspects of the scenario. In no time we glide into the front emerald lawn facing the antique tan and square Victorian.

Alejandro Murguía is sitting on the bed with his back to the windows. He is a lean young man. He reminds me of a campesino that I met in Chiapas who said he loved to be alone in the fields of maíz and that he wasn't himself in the big towns like San Cristóbal. Alejandro is dark. He has the aura of a human lizard dressed in a silk suit. He appears elegant, motionless, and foreboding.

He lures out a few syllables: "How's it going, man?" I decide to do one of my one-word Bogart moves: "Suave."

No one is speaking, although I can see through the corner of my eye that Tomás is gesturing wildly to La Geraldine about the film project.

The heat is unbearable. Everything has taken on a slick brush stroke of thin oil. Even the walls suddenly appear with a new glazy coat. We seem to be rotating around each other like carousel dolls.

La Geraldine comes over and slowly hovers over Alejandro. I want to think that they are lovers, but a distinct feeling takes hold of me; all of us look so out of place here. Alejandro stops the daze: "Look, why don't you come up to the city? We just took over a building; a place for artists and writers to live and work and get it together. ¿Qué te parece?"

Everyone joins in and talks about another battle plan in the Mission District of San Francisco. Alejandro mentions his essay on political theatre soon to be published by Pocho-Che Editions. There's only time for a cigarette, a few gestures. Suddenly, it is over.

I take another hit of mineral water.

I think about heading back to Venice. This old Victorian is a mystery. Who lives here, anyway? Maybe the basement leads to an underground chamber and the secret opening to one of the seven magical caves of Aztlán. Or maybe it's a classy depot for winos and Movement gente rented out by a Chicano Studies professor with tenure. Tomás and I walk out to the front porch. I look back. Alejandro seems to have moved only a few inches; you can see his steely profile against the brilliant white curtains. He studies Geraldine as she speaks. It is about 2:30 in the afternoon. No one is out.

La Cucaracha looks funny parked next to the plump line of 1952 Plymouths.

I can feel the giant tan checker-piece looming behind us as Tomás puts the car into third gear.

Los buenos indicios

Fausto Avendaño

Tu nombre completo . . . Henrique Estrada Díaz, si omites los apellidos inútiles. Eres hijo natural de un empresario de teatro y de una actriz, antigua intérprete de la canción española mexicana. Según cuentan, fue una mujer bella y difícil, pero de indudable talento. Aún te acuerdas de sus triunfantes "jiras" por España y las Américas . . . Lástima que muriera en flor de la juventud, en un accidente automovilístico—¡qué banal! Tú tenías diez años en aquel entonces; si hubiera vivido . . .

Pero tú has sabido abrirte camino . . . sin ninguna ayuda. Te forjaste, te moldeaste y te hiciste un hombre de bien. Eso nadie te lo puede quitar. Eres periodista y actor; sobre todo actor . . . Y de los buenos, aunque este miserable Hollywood no te lo reconozca. La verdad es que aún no se te ha presentado la oportunidad que esperas, pero ésta llegará tarde o temprano. ¡Tiene que llegar!

Todavía luces joven, todo mundo te lo dice—cumpliste los treinta y dos el mes pasado—, pero no eres tonto . . . Comprendes que no hay tiempo que perder. Sabes muy bien que es ahora o nunca, antes que aparezcan las canas, las arrugas . . . o peor, ¡la temida calvicie! Si vas a llegar a la cúspide, ¡hay que comenzar ahora mismo!

Eres un hombre casado, claro. La vida no se pasa sin compañera . . . Ella también es actriz, hija de un cantante famoso allá en México. Carmen se llama y es un ejemplo magnífico de nuestra belleza femenina. ¡Qué cutis aperlado y suave! ¡Qué ojos castaños! Y el cuerpo: el de una bailarina andaluza! Pero, vamos, deja de pensar en esas cosas. Tienes el asunto de siempre. Hay que ir al café de rigor, el indispensable . . . donde todo mundo te conoce y te saluda. El lugar donde se reunen los actores . . . los consagrados y los que, como tú, buscan esa huidiza oportunidad.

Al llegar, pedirás, como de costumbre, tu agua Perrier y una ensalada de camarón; después cambiarás la copa reglamentaria de Porto. Tras una ligera charla en español con el cantinero—un mucha-

cho de Guadalajara—volverás a tu coche para emprender el largo
viaje a casa.

Ya se te ha ocurrido que esta rutina es una fatiga . . . Tal vez lo
sea, pero ¿qué remedio? Hay que seguirla. No hay que desviarse del
camino . . . Cuando se quiere triunfar, cuando se anhela llegar a lo más
alto, no hay sacrificio imposible. Hay que estar siempre disponible
. . . porque la suerte llega sin ningún anuncio. Así les ha pasado a
otros . . . La oferta de empleo les ha caído de repente, ¡cuando menos
la esperaban!

Ah . . . si la Fortuna te sonriera . . . Si se te diera la oportunidad,
como se les dio a los latinos que han triunfado en el cine, tú serías de
los mejores. Sabes que es posible. Allí están los ejemplos de Raquel
Welch, de Eric Estrada (tu tocayo), de Rita Hayworth, de Fernando
Lamas, de Dolores del Río, de Ricardo Montalbán, y de sabrá Dios
cuántos otros. Con los *stage names* ya no se sabe quiénes son de origen
hispano.

Hasta ahora no has tenido suerte . . . Reconócelo. ¿Para qué te
vas a engañar? Por una u otra razón te han pasado por alto y escogido a
otros. Tienes que ver las cosas tal como son: el papel más grande que
desempeñaste fue el de oficial español en una película de Zorro. Pero,
vamos, tampoco no te desalientes. La suerte tiene que cambiar. Es
caprichosa, pero a todos les toca tarde o temprano.

Al bajar del automóvil atisbas un billete . . . Sí, ¡es un billete! Está
entre otros papeles arrollados por el viento contra el poste de un farol.
Te acercas y lo recoges. ¡Es una nota de cien dólares! Está clara la
estampa de Benjamín Franklin. Vaya que suerte. Ya te tocaba. No es
uno de a mil, pero de todos modos no cae mal.

Entras en el restaurante con una sonrisa en los labios y el dueño
te saluda de mano con toda cordialidad. Esto de ninguna forma te
extraña. El lo hace siempre. ¡Y por qué no! Eres un tipo agradable,
indiscutiblemente guapo y de intachables modales. Claro que te ha de
tratar bien. Al fin y al cabo, eres uno de los elementos que contribuye
al ambiente del sitio. Tienes el porte interesante de actor. No es por
nada que los turistas te han confundido con Jason Douglas y Frank
Cappola.

Saludas a varios concurrentes, entre ellos actores y actrices de
renombre. Tú no los quieres mal porque ellos por lo menos te respe-
tan. "Henry, ¿cómo estás?" te dicen y te aprietan la mano. "¿Qué hay

de nuevo en tu vida?" Tú ya estás acostrumbrado a este trato. Es
natural que te estimen y te admiren . . . No hay por qué ser modesto.
Sabes muy bien que tienes el don de gente, sobre todo, cuando se trata
de mujeres. ¡Qué va! Ya has dejado de contar las aspirantes a actriz que
se mueren por ti. Pero tú has sabido zafarte . . . y no tan sólo por serle
fiel a tu mujer, sino porque no estás dispuesto a perder el tiempo. El
que anhela el triunfo no se mete con novatas. Eso no conduce a
nungún sitio. Ahora, si se interesara por ti alguna actriz verdadera,
claro está que no titubearías, por más que quieras a tu mujer. Hay que
reconocer que de esas relaciones salen hechos estrellas luminosas
desconocidos hasta sin talento. Ah, si hubiese quién te prote-
giera . . . ¡Qué no harías por conseguir la fama! Claro que no dejarías
a tu mujer—seguirías queriéndola, como siempre. Tendrías, como
bien dicen, un sencillo y discreto *affair*, nada más.

Te sientas a la mesa habitual y pides tu almuerzo. Mientras
esperas, vuelves el pensamiento a tu mujer . . . Lamentas decirlo,
pero las cosas no marchan bien entre tú y ella. El problema está en que
tu esposa ya se dio por vencida. Tiene veinte y siete años y dice que
quiere una vida normal. Se cansó de los enfadosos y fríos *auditions* y se
puso a trabajar en algo más productivo, según ella. Te rogó que dejaras
la ilusión, pero tú . . . tú no puedes. Mientras haya una esperanza, por
más pequeña que sea . . . Lo que más te molesta es que tenga un
empleo—un buen trabajo, como dice ella . . . Es secretaria bilingüe y,
claro, tiene mejor salario que tú.

Y tú, ¿a qué te dedicas? Escribes artículos, cuentos y crónicas para
el periódico de lengua hispana. Es cierto que no te pagan bien
. . . pero esa actividad, hay que reconocerlo, te conserva en forma y te
permite, sobre todo, un horario flexible. También, de vez en cuando,
te compremetes a participar en alguna obrita representada en los
teatros regionales. Tampoco te aporta gran ganancia, pero eso sí, ¡te da
vida! El que es actor tiene que ejercer su arte.

El mesero te trae la ensalada y te dispones a comer cuando divisas a
lo lejos el rostro de Jason Douglas . . . Sí . . . es él. Tú conoces,
aunque ligeramente. Viene acompañdo de Elizabeth Woods . . . Sí, es
ella. Parece que se dirigen a tu mesa. ¿O te equivocas?

—¡Henry!— te llama Jason. Tú te pones de pie en el acto, como si
estuvieras ante la pareja real, y saludas con tu acostumbrada amabi-
lidad. El actor te habla con animación, mientras tú devoras con los

ojos a la mujer. Consideras que ha perdido la lozanía de la juventud, pero en su lugar encuentras un bouquet de encantos femeninos engendrado por los años. No cabe duda . . . ostenta una gracia delicada que sólo la experiencia de las cosas y el caudal confieren. ¡Qué hembra! ¡Y qué historia! ¡La pasión ante todo!

Jason Douglas te presenta y ella te dirige la palabra como si fueras amigo de mucho tiempo. Te dice que tuvo la ocasión de verte en una película—la de Zorro—y cree haber percibido harto talento. Por ello se propuso conocerte e invitarte a un *soirée* que brindaba al equipo de su última película. Tú aceptas encantado y ella añade que tendrá el gusto de presentarte a varios de sus amigos, entre ellos a Jack Marcus, el célebre cineasta. No cabes en ti de contento, pero disimulas. Les invitas un cóctel—al cabo traes el billete de a cien—, pero ellos declinan. Tienen que estar en el *set* dentro de media hora. Se despiden y, al alejarse, Jason te guiña el ojo.

¡Qué fortuna! Hoy es el día de la suerte. Ya lo habías oído tantas veces: cuando las cosas se mejoran y se halla uno al borde de la prosperidad, todo cambia de golpe, aun cuando la esperanza haya comenzado a menguar.

El apetito ya te abandonó, pero allí tienes la ensalada y te pones a comer . . . En ese momento llega el *maître de table* y te entrega el teléfono.

—Un telefonema para Ud. Le das las gracias y sonríes satisfecho. Ya estás acostumbrado a este exceso de servicio. Sabes que el dueño lo hace para impresionar a los turistas. Te pones el auricular al oído, esperando oír la voz de tu mujer . . . pero no, no es ella, una voz de hombre . . . ¡Es una llamada de MG Studios! Te han escogido para uno de los papeles principales junto al actor Jason Douglas, ¡al que acabas de ver! La decisión ha tardado mucho porque no dependía tan sólo del director sino de un comité formado para ese efecto. Vieron el video de tu ensayo—el que hiciste hace un mes—y creen que tú harás mejor el papel. Se trata del rival de Douglas (en la película), un personaje que debe ser guapo, viril y, a la vez, algo simpático, a pesar de ser el villano. A la orden, dices; te presentarás en el *set* el lunes a las nueve en punto. Claro está . . . no faltarás. Cuelgas.

¡Qué suerte! Otro indicio . . . Ahora sí . . . ¿Qué duda puede haber? Serás un actor hecho y derecho. Ya está en la suerte . . . Ha de ser obra de Elizabeth Woods. No cabe duda . . . ¡Ella busca a quien proteger!

Se te ocurre llamarla a tu mujer. A alguien le tienes que contar tu buena fortuna. Marcas los números precipitadamente. Ella contesta y te dice que no la llames al trabajo . . . el jefe ya se está fijando. Que se vaya al diablo el jefe, piensas y le dices que tienes una noticia muy importante. En seguida desembuchas. Fuiste escogido para una gran película con Jason Douglas . . . Serás el rival. Nada de papelillos de mala muerte. ¡Es todo un papel! Ella no sabe qué decir. Apenas lo puede creer. Nunca pensó que fuera posible. Tú sonríes y le aseguras que es cuestión de destino. Cuando las puertas se abren, en un santiamén quedan de par en par. Le dices que si tú subes, si tú triunfas, ella subirá contigo . . . Ella está emocionada, pero incrédula y tú se lo vuelves a aseverar. Esta noche irán a celebrar tu estrella en algún restaurante de primera. Tú pagarás, insistes. Para eso traes con qué. Te despides.

De nuevo te pones a comer la ensalada, pero no te entra la lechuga y los camarones se te atoran en la garganta. Definitivamente careces de apetito. Es mejor pedir la cuenta y pagarla. Son diez dólares con cincuenta y nueve centavos. Dejas quince y te marchas. Aún te quedan ciento veintitantos en la billetera. Más que suficiente para una cena con buen vino del país.

Al salir se te acerca una aspirante a actriz . . . se llama Rachel. Es rubia, un poco narigona, pero tiene un cuerpo que asesina. Te pide que te tomes un trago con ella . . . quiere un poco de compañía. Con toda certidud, necesita desahogarse . . . Pobre muchacha. Tú la comprendes. Esto de buscar el camino de la fama no es juego de niños. Te disculpas, pero hoy no puedes . . . Tal vez mañana. Hoy te han llamado para un ensayo y no debes demorarte. Lo sientes . . . Le das un beso en la mejilla y sales con paso apresurado.

Hoy es el día que comienza de verdad tu carrera de *star*; está en la suerte, doña Fortuna te sonrió, al fin. ¡Hoy es el mejor día de tu vida!

Te acercas al coche . . . Vas a abrir la puerta del lado del conductor . . . Pero ¿qué haces, insensato? ¿No ves lo que viene?

El camión no pudo parar a tiempo. Los tres testigos dijeron que la víctima andaba medio dormido, con una sonrisa ensimismada, como en un ensueño. El camionero frenó, pero no pudo evitar el accidente. El golpe lo aventó a unos cuatro metros de distancia. No hubo más. Henry Estrada Díaz murió instantáneamente. Dejó de existir en el mejor día de su vida.

Sunland

Gloria Velásquez Treviño

Tuve la sensación de haber pasado por este momento en otra ocasión, de haber pisado cuidadosamente, primero con el pie izquierdo, luego con el derecho hasta llegar a su lado y plantarle ese mismo beso amargo en su cachete indígena. Sería *déjà vu*, como decían los gringos, quizás, o tal vez otra vaga ilusión de la vida, sí, eso debía ser.

—Pase mi'jita, pase— me dijo apretándome la mano. —Está chico el traile pero me gusta. Me recuerda mis días de borreguero, pasaba mucho tiempo en unos más chicos que éstos. No, tú no te acuerdas, estaban bien chicos tú y Antonio pero tu mami los traiba a visitarme.

Escuché la voz de Tonio y lo vi allí agachado jugando con sus soldaditos verdes. Quise resistir, quedarme con esa imagen frágil del pasado, pero la voz melodiosa de mi abuelo me jalaba del lado de Tonio.

—¿Cómo te has sentido hija? ¿Por qué no te acompañó Raúl?

"Raúl", suspiré sin contestarle, recordando su amarga presencia aquella noche cuando sentí por la última vez el dolor de sus manos que bruscamente me acariciaban los senos hasta llegar al bulto que cargaba dentro de mí. Para qué decirle que ya pasaban meses desde que lo había visto. Mejor mentir. ¿Acaso no era la vida una bola de mentiras, una bola enorme que rodaba y rodaba, apachurrando a todo lo que encontraba en su camino?

Me vi levantarme; escuché el sonido de mis pasos sobre el piso de hule de la cocina. Ojeaba la pequeña estufa, los muebles, las paredes sucias, manchadas de tanto sufrir como su huésped. La imagen de Raúl, de su sexo duro, se mezclaba con la de Tonio y los soldaditos verdes.

—Ven hija, siéntate. Anda, mientras te traigo unas galletas que hice, son como las que te hacía la nana.

Fue entonces cuando se me vino a la memoria aquel día y la vi allí sentada en su rincón como bulto, estropeada, perdida en su propio mundo. Esa noche nos había rogado mi mamá que se la cuidáramos por un rato mientras ellos salían a pasearse, pero se lo habíamos negado; yo me quería ir a un sock-hop con Mercitas y Tonio estaba apurado por irse con sus amigos. Por eso, cuando se la tuvieron que llevar en la madrugada casi muerta al hospital para que los médicos la examinaran como cadáver y pudieran confirmar su hipótesis, lloré, maldije, me rasguñé las entrañas hasta sentir la sangre escurrir y caer en gotas gruesas sobre mis pies. Pero Tonio no había dicho nada, ni un suspiro se le había escapado aun cuando la maldita enfermedad empezaba a escaparse por las cuencas de la nana, deteniéndose por fin con el último suspiro. Desde ese día, lo sentí diferente, como si él mismo hubiera probado la muerte.

—Anda, hija, come—. Cogí la galleta que me ofrecía. —Quiero que conozcas a mi vecino, también mexicano— me dijo y acercándose a la puerta —Ssssh, compadre, venga.

Apareció un señor moreno y a pesar de su cuerpo delgado y jorobado, sentí la presencia de lo que antes había sido un hombre fuerte, noble como aquellos caciques indígenas del pasado. Me vi extenderle la mano y me apretaron unos dedos largos que no parecían querer soltarme como si lo ahogara el río y solamente yo lo pudiera socorrer. Le retiré la mano bruscamente.

—Siéntese a platicar, compadre.

—No puedo quedarme compadre. Espero a mi Jenny, 'orita llega.

Se le atoraban las palabras; sería por esa maldita flaqueza que se extendía por todo su cuerpo. Quise huir, esconderme como había hecho aquella desolada mañana cuando la voz de mi mamá me suplicaba que fuera a despedirme de Antonio.

—Está seguro que no es a la gringa Dorothy que espera— le contestó el Dalín, guiñándome el ojo.

Una risa suave, melódica como la antigua poesía que los indígenas habían creado para adorar a sus dioses antes de que los atrapara la historia como había hecho con este mexicano y muchos otros, le sacudió todo su cuerpo hasta que por fin se escapó libre al aire. La vi resonar contra las paredes, las ventanas, hasta que por fin cayó muerta a mi lado. Estiré la mano para tocarla, pero algo me detuvo.

—Ay, don Luis, como es usté— Había volteado a verme y por un instante me vi parada a su lado arriba de la inmensa pirámide del sol escuchando los antiguos cantos de los dioses, sintiéndome libre y llena de esperanzas. —Bueno señorita, mucho gusto. Más tarde nos vemos, don Luis.

Se había desvanecido la risa y ansiosamente empecé a buscarla.
—Pobre compadre, esa vale mierda hija que tiene, viene nomás para
quitarle su cheque. ¿Y viste que tan flaco está? No quiere comer bien.
Yo le doy de la comida que cocino porque esa porquería que le train las
viejitas del Salvation Army no sirve. De todos modos, come poco.
Temo que se vaya a enfermar y se lo lleven al resthome, ni inglés sabe.
Yo que tan mal hablo el inglés, hasta le gano.
Por dondequiera buscaba aquella risa pura, lejana, aun en los ojos
nublados de mi abuelo. Imposible. Ya no existía. Había que cambiar de
temas, sí, eso debería hacer.

—¿Cómo está doña Soledad? ¿Todavía se hablan cada día?—
balbuceé, acordándome de su respuesta el día que le había sugerido
que se casara con ella: "No, mi'jita, yo nunca volveré a casarme. Jamás
habrá otra mujer como tu nana y al cabo yo no aguantaría a esa plebe
que tiene".
Respiró profundamente antes de contestarme. —Pobre Soledad,
desde que le dio el último ataque, se quedó paralizada. Según dice el
chisme, han regresado todos porque la vecina que la cuidaba ya no
puede con ella. . . .

Habían llegado durante la noche, resbalándose silenciosamente
como culebras por todo el camino de tierra hasta llegar a la casita de
doña Soledad. En un rincón de la pequeña cocina habían aventado sus
maletas sin preocuparse por colgar su ropa o siquiera sacar el cepillo de
dientes. Mecánica y cuidadosamente se habían abrazado, una palma-
dita en la espalda, pos como estás gorda, debe ser ese aire californiano,
¿que no haces al jog? Y los demás pensando, viejo panzón, nomás viene
a sacarle dinero para mantener a esa puta. La gorda dominaba la
conversación con pláticas de su hijo, el computer engineer, de su hija,
la concert pianist, de su pet poodle, Fifi, y mientras tanto, todos se
fijaban en sus zapatos baratos, su pelo pintado, y su Playtex girdle que a
cada rato se le subía, pellizcándola y haciéndola rascarse las nalgas. A la
flaca se le atoraban las palabras, po-po-bre-a-má—y. Cada vez que
hablaba se escapaban unas carcajadas del grupo. Al verla palidecer y
empezar a retorcerse con temblones fuertes, se callaban todos. El más
joven, hombre con bastante educación, echaba chiste tras chiste con
intención de romper el silencio de envidia y enojos que habían creado
entre sí mismos, pero al ver que nadie le hacía caso, cambiaba de

temas: ¿Vieron *That's Incredible* anoche? Salió un hombre que podía soplar 100 bubbles cada segundo.

Al terminarse la happy reunion, los cuatro hijos procedieron en fila hacia la recámara de doña Soledad. Permanecía extendida en la camita tapada con una colcha gruesa y lo único que se revelaba debajo de su camiseta blanca eran los indicios de unos senos, secos y apachurrados por los años. A su lado quemaba una vela de la Virgen de Guadalupe cuyo olor se mezclaba con el de los orines anaranjados del vacinero que quedaba al pie de la cama. Tenía los ojos abiertos con la mirada fijada en la pared como si estuviera revisando los retratos que la rodeaban, el de su esposo, que, con los bigotes negros y su sombrero de paja, se parecía a uno de esos antiguos oficiales de la Revolución Mexicana. Al otro lado, colgaba la vieja foto de su matrimonio. ¿Recordaría a aquella muchacha joven vestida de blanco y repleta de esperanzas? ¿O pensaría en el día que murió su esposo lejos de ella en aquel cuarto vacío que olía a medicinas y enfermos?

Hablando en voz bajita, se acomodaban a su alrededor, pobre amá, que flaca está, decía el mayor mientras encendía su Muriel cigar. La gorda, soplando a un lado el humo que empezaba a llenar el cuarto, le acomodaba la colcha, ¿Necesita algo amá? ¿Le puedo traer un cafecito? La flaca, apretándose el paño contra sus narices agudas, le acariciaba las trenzas largas mientras que el joven murmuraba, pos a todos nos toca, *C'est la vie*, ¿que no? Después de quedarse parados quince minutos a su lado (y habían sido exactamente quince porque había sonado "Beep, beep, beep" el reloj del joven) regresaron los cuatro hermanos a la sala para finalizar sus planes.

—Quesque la vecina ya no puede con ella, así que tenemos que decidir algo.

El hijo mayor, medio pelón, se rascaba desesperadamente la barriga y después de una larga pausa, —Es mejor que se venga conmigo, que muera en su país.

—¿Y qué va a hacer allá tan lejos? Yo me la podría llevar a California por un tiempo. Tengo una casa grande, bi-level, three bathrooms. The girls would love it.

—Estás loca. Tú ni para limpiarte el culero tienes tiempo, siempre pa'llí, pa'cá con ese bonche.

—En mi opinión, Happy Haven es el lugar para ella. Tienen air conditioning, saunas privadas para los viejitos y bingo games every Wednesday night!

Este huero, pero sí que está retardao, más burro que el burro, pensó el pelón al encenderse otro puro. La flaca quiso expresar su opinión, me-me-pa-re-re-ce, pero otra vez se dejó dominar por los temblones y la toz. Avergonzada, huyó a la cocina. De vez en cuando, uno de ellos se deshacía del grupo para asomarse al cuarto de la anciana. Pero por más que trataran de quedarse a su lado, recordando esa dulce imagen de su mamá moliendo maíz con toda su destreza indígena, el olor del vacinero los sacaba huyendo del cuarto.

—Tenemos que hacer una decisión— repitió bostezando la gorda sin quitar la vista de sus dedos hinchados que adornaba con el más reciente color de Avon, Purple Magic —y tiene que ser pronto porque mi hija tiene un recital el lunes.

De repente, saltó el joven sobre la mesa. —I've got it! Una lotería, ¿por qué no tenemos una lotería y así dejamos que el pueblo haga la decisión? Venderemos billetes y el que gana decidirá su destino.—Se rascó la cabeza. (Había momentos en que le sorprendía su propia inteligencia.)

Dejaron escapar unos sollozos de alivio; sí, buena idea, de algo le sirvió estudiar al huero, que decida la gente de Sunland.

Se decía que desde 1848, se había tapado un lado del sol y por más que trataran los científicos no podían encontrar una hipótesis que explicara la falta de luz en algunos de los barrios de Sunland. Pasaban horas, días, meses examinando el sol por sus inmensos telescopios hasta poder identificar los movimientos precisos del sol. Hubo un año en que habían calculado la posición exacta del sol al instante que soltara su canto el gallo. Pero la oscuridad permanecía y a lo largo del tiempo se dieron cuenta de que este fenómeno existía por todo el suroeste. Por fin, decidieron abandonar sus teorías e instrumentos inútiles y aceptar la idea de que donde hubiera pobreza siempre habría oscuridad. Había llegado aquella tarde en pleno día y lentamente se había acomodado en los rincones, en los muros, aun en los rostros humildes de la gente de Sunland que poco a poco se acostumbraban a la idea de vivir sin luz. Para qué tener cortinas, lámparas si la oscuridad entraba por dondequiera. Dormían con ella, hasta se sentaban juntos a la mesa. Sólo en las vecindades al otro lado del pueblo brillaba tan fuerte el sol que, según contaban, tenían que usar palas para recoger las rosas enormes que se caían de los rosales que florecían las 24 horas al día.

Ya hacía meses que los habitantes de Sunland habían notado la enredadera mágica que lentamente se subía por todas las paredes de la casita de doña Soledad. Convencidos de que eran las esperanzas, (¿pos cómo fregaos podría crecer una planta donde no había luz?) habían ido algunos a escondidas y escarbado cuidadosamente hasta sacarse un pedazo de la planta milagrosa. Desgraciadamente, al tratar de crecerla en sus yardas, echándole agua cien veces al día, se les había muerto. A Arsenio lo había dominado tanto la curiosidad que había sacado los antiguos science books de Esperanza para tratar de encontrar alguna información científica sobre la planta mágica. En cambio, Leticia, que pensaba que todo en la vida se relacionaba al cuerpo y a la salud, la había arrancado unas hojas y las había hervido para un té. Pero al probarlo, se quiso ahogar. Asustada, mejor decidió abandonar su proyecto, como lo había hecho su marido, y olvidarse de la yerba misteriosa.

Las noticias de la lotería pronto corrieron de boca en boca. Muy picados, los habitantes de Sunland se pusieron en cola durante toda una semana para poder conseguir un billete. Estaba dividida la gente; algunos seguían la opinión del joven, y está acabada, mejor que se la lleven al resthome. Otros con su corazón mexicano gritaban, ¡Viva México! ¡Que muera en su país, que se la lleve el pelón! Los más progresistas favorecían el aire californiano donde se decía que habían tantos avances tecnológicos, que quizás pudieran ponerle partes biónicas a la viuda, tenía razón la gorda. Pasaban muchas horas discutiendo el caso en los campos, en el correo, en los excusados oscuros tratando de decidir el destino de doña Soledad.

Había llegado la fecha para escoger el billete ganador. Las cámaras de Channel 7 rodeaban el escenario, frenéticamente tratando de entrevistar a la gente de Sunland que ansiosamente esperaba saber los resultados de la lotería. De repente, apareció un trueno en el cielo oscuro que fue seguido por otros aún más fuertes. Los habitantes de Sunland, sorprendidos por la luz que producían los truenos, dejaron soltar sus billetes y con gritos de Ave María Purísima, se soltaron corriendo a sus hogares. Los hijos de doña Soledad, también asustados por la tormenta inesperada, huyeron al lado de la gorda. Acomodándose con insultos y pellizcos debajo de su inmenso paraguas californiano dejaron que el viento los soplara hacia la casa de su mamá donde los dejó caer en bola sobre el apestoso lodo. Al levantarse, soltaron un grito: la casita estaba completamente tapada por una enredadera gigantesca que subía hasta perderse en las nubes.

Tuvieron que esperar hasta que cesara la inundación diluviana antes de reunir a toda la gente de Sunland. Juntaron machetes y bulldozers batallando en el lodo por muchos días hasta que por fin abrieron un paso al interior de la planta mágica, pero al pisar adentro, lo único que hallaron fue el vacinero de doña Soledad.

Me vi abrazarlo. En ese momento exacto sentí un olor fuerte y otra vez tuve esa loca sensación de haber sentido la misma náusea en otra ocasión, de haber sentido el mismo asco al ver los orines sucios de la nana. "Estás loca", me dije, "necesitas descansar".

Fue cuando me subía al carro, que lo vi acercarse al banco y tocarle el hombro suavemente a Pedro que se había quedado dormido esperando a su hija. Todos esperando algo, ese algo que no llegaba. "Some day my ship will come in", me decía mi papá.

Payback
(Dirty for Dirty)

Patricio F. Vargas

Wilshire Boulevard was bustling with people glad to be out during the lunch hour after a week of unusually heavy rain in Los Angeles. The wide, fancy street was crowded with people, mostly women, animated by the marvelous, pleasant change in weather: bees streaming out of dark, humid hives, into brilliant sunshine, coming alive.

Women seductively, attractively dressed, glad to expose their femininity in revealing clothing. Sexy shoes and alluring dresses with lively, inviting faces, their eyes darting, looking, addressing, flirting— just great to be out walking, letting men look at them. The two men, pretending nonchalance, using their peripheral vision, swiveling from side to side of the street, checking out all the possibilities for a flirtation or just an eyeful of female.

The blue pickup glided slowly down Wilshire towards the tallest of the buildings, on the 3400 block.

"You know what the son of a whore has done for me? For $1,000 I've gotten a receipt and a letter! ¡Hijo de su pinche, puta, perra madre! He made me so many promises. And to think I trusted that fucking lawyer!" the squat Mexican troglodyte said animatedly to the driver, another Mexican, who sat with an intense, preoccupied air as he drove and enjoyed the women on the busy boulevard.

"He said he could get all my family documented for only $2,300, and all I got in two years was a receipt!"

The driver, nodding in understanding and faint boredom at hearing the complaining repetition . . . rehearsing in his mind what his strategy was going to be once he sized up the lawyer. The simple peasant's litany and pleas for help were beginning to weary him.

They parked at the rear of the tall, ritzy, imposing building and headed for the 25th floor.

"You should have seen how well he treated me, had the two kiss-ass secretaries translate for me every minute . . . God damn bitches, they pretend they're not Mexican, but their assholes are as

black as mine . . . and once I handed him the $1,000 I never heard
from him again!" The beefy man, grossly overweight at 5 feet 5 inches
and 250 pounds, kept up his running commentary. An ambulatory
washing machine of a man, his thick arms and thicker body thrashing
through the air, trying to keep up with his rescuer; bull-like neck,
powerful shoulders and trapezius bulging, years of plastering made
visible in his bunched-up muscles as he trundled along.

Taking the elevator, they continued to speak in Spanish, discon-
certing the other passengers, who outwardly pretended not to hear,
but who inwardly strained their ears to catch the meaning of the alien
sounds, recoiling slightly at the foreign look and sound of the two
chattering Mexicans in the small space.

"Wanna see a guy named Phil, works here," said the younger man
to the caged-in receptionist, and they were both admitted into the
winding recesses of the plush law offices of twelve lawyers who had
their full names inscribed in the tall wall of the wide, lush lobby,
crowding each other out of the huge brass plate.

Philip Rombly III (as his business card read) was taller than the
taller Mexican and wore a black suit. His thick, curly, dark hair
surrounded a soft, unformed, tanned face that had a little swarthy
radish for a nose; small, blue, darting eyes that stood still and widened
for emphasis completed his face.

"Manny Rodríguez! Glad to see you! What's up?" asked the lawyer
in a silly, inappropriate way, of the peasant who stood in the doorway,
unsure as to the strange etiquette of these white men who smiled and
shook your hand warmly while you tried to look angry and offended.

"Came to get Manuel's $1,000," said the younger Mexican with-
out preamble to the surprised lawyer.

"Now I told him that I needed a letter of employment from his
employer before I could start the citizenship procedure. Tell him
that."

The Mexican walked to the large easy chair opposite the lawyer's
desk and sat down without invitation. Manuel followed suit.

"It's been two years and you never moved on the case. Now he
wants his money back and we'll leave," he said, ignoring the lawyer's
request.

"I can't move without that letter, you tell him that. It's all his
doing. I've done a lotta work on his case. I've put in a lot of time."

Putting his hand on the phone as he talked, he put on his professional voice and asked his secretary to bring in the "Rodríguez file."

They both ignored Manuel . . . he wasn't there. Manuel, the aggrieved party, sat silently, only half understanding the goings-on . . . a spectator in his own fight. He understood bricks, mortar and wood; they were honest, with straightforward natures, as long as you followed basic rules of nature and geometry.

Building materials had a noble simplicity; they were not out to trick or deceive you. Although some were easier to work with than others, you could always trust them to behave in a thoroughly predictable manner. Materials were so strong yet so vulnerable if only you knew their secrets. It was a matter of contradictions and opposite natures: his hands, though horny, were soft compared to wood, yet he could bend steel and order it around; concrete, in its liquid state, was a hapless gruel manipulated into any shape or container, but once hardened it became as immutable as any thousand-year-old rock. Wood and tile became plastic in his hands, yielding beauty and utility.

Soft hands enslaving hard wood and metal. Some materials were more slavish than others, but all surrendered their strength and might to the seductive cunning of manually applied physics, persuading, convincing them.

Materials he could understand, but men, who knew them? How could you tell? What was so right for one was nearly death to another. It was not possible to understand men.

His rescuer was a learned man, cultured; he could even speak English and write. And yet he seemed almost a hoodlum as he addressed the lawyer, so disrespectful! Even though he himself felt angry and wronged by the crafty lawyer, a man had to behave according to courtesy, even in anger, not like this, like a commoner! If only he could speak English, if only he could fight for himself, if only he knew what to do.

The secretary politely knocked, entered, and handed her boss the file.

"See, look here," he said, pointing to the bulging file the secretary brought in. "It's all there."

"We want the $1,000, not talk. I've already blown two hours on you; I can't wait anymore. We're going to lean on you if you don't deliver." The Mexican slouched, quietly menacing.

"I don't want trouble, but look at the work I've done. Can't we compromise, say $500? Tell him."

"Phil, you made a few calls, wrote a few notes maybe, that's about all. This guy's a working slob; he lives from hand to mouth, after busting his balls on any construction job he can find. He does real work; you're a lawyer." The Mexican took off his dark glasses with deliberate, slow movements as he sat up in the large chair, coming from his recumbent, leisurely slouch.

"This guy uses his body like a cheap tool every day. Parts of his body are older than the rest from overuse. He's 54 and all he has is a twenty-year-old truck and second-rate tools and you want to take him. He travels back and forth from Mexico without papers, doesn't speak English, and because you treated him nice after he put in doors for you, he thought he could trust you. I'm going to give you a hundred bucks for your work. Give him back $900 and we're even," said the Mexican, never looking at the apprehensive lawyer, speaking quietly into his lap.

The lawyer's mind raced, weighing the pros and cons; caught between his not wanting to "lose" $900 and the unknown fear that was overcoming his sense of economy.

He felt guilty and threatened. The work he had done on the case was minimal and he had never been so bluntly confronted. The Mexican's cold, indifferent manner had penetrated his social shell of self-confidence. It was eerie. The stocky, English-speaking Mexican reminded him of the mean neighborhood greaseballs he had grown up with in Pomona. That quiet, indirect, cold aggression that would suddenly explode in mindless fury. They didn't seem to care. If you were friends, they would slash their bellies open for you. But if you messed with their sisters, they would look up your entire family.

On the other hand, they were so dumb and fearful of authority. They would respectfully retreat before any show of authority or official sanction. They always seemed apologetic and smiley, especially the older ones. It was the younger ones that seemed to have a vague grasp of their rights. Still, you never knew. He might be able to talk sense into the spick, but he seemed so remote. These guys were primitive.

"Look, maybe we can talk about this," he said to the reclining menace. "I don't have any money right now."

"How much you got in your wallet? Take it out!"

Mechanically, realizing the Mexican was implacable, he took the wallet out and held out for all to see the $40.00 he had.

"See, I have no money!" he said, realizing his hopes for negotiations were evaporating.

"What about those rings? Take them off. How much are your teeth worth?"

The lawyer felt his composure fall from him; he was being robbed in his own office and he could not stop himself from cooperating. He felt ten years old again, being shaken down by neighborhood spicks. Oh, God.

"I can't take them off. I never do," he said, nearly whining, extending his large, soft hands, palms down, towards the Mexican, and then brandishing them like shields, waggling his large wooly head for emphasis, his eyes widening.

School had let out an hour ago and his mother would be searching the route to school. I got to get home.

"All right. Make out a check for $900."

"I haven't got it," squeaked out Phil, against the wall, his heart thundering.

"You don't seem to appreciate the gravity of your situation, Phil. I don't want to hassle with you; I now know what you look like, you know what I look like, and you'll never see me again. I don't ever want to see you again," the Mexican said, his droopy moustache making his face appear melancholy with his slow, soft, menacing voice contradicting his looks.

Phil scrambled in his mind for the checkbook, but in reality his ego moved slowly and calmly and wrote out the check in his large, tidy handwriting.

The Mexicans took the check and left.

The lawyer took the rest of the day off.

La última despedida

Ana María Salazar

El encargado de comunicarle a mi nana las tristes noticias fue mi padre. Mi nana estaba acomodada en su silla de ruedas, se veía frágil, pero hermosa. Vestía una bata rosada, color que ella consideraba indecente para una mujer de su edad. Pero la única forma de soportar el verano era llevar ropa ligera y de colores claros. Mi padre se veía fuera de lugar en su traje negro. No hallaba las palabras correctas para decirle a mi nana las malas noticias. Por fin mi padre titubeó y dijo: "Mamá, papá se ha ido". "Este condenado de tu padre", replicó mi nana, "¿por qué no avisó que iba a salir del hospital?" Su cara estaba fruncida del enojo. Mi padre palideció y de nuevo intentó, "Mamá, usted no me entiende. Papá se ha ido de a buenas". "Bueno, pero ¿por qué no avisó?" volvió a repetir mi nana con los ojos perplejos. Finalmente, mi padre con el llanto en la cara murmuró: "Mamá, papá ha muerto".

El silencio se rompió con un aullido inhumano que provenía de mi nana. Todos los que nos encontrábamos en el cuarto nos unimos a sus agudos y descontrolados gritos de dolor. Mi nana nunca volvería a usar colores, de ahora en adelante sólo se vestiría de negro.

Yo tenía 15 años cuando murió mi tata, y era la primera vez que sentía la muerte tan de cerca. Su cuerpo estaba envuelto en las sábanas verdes del hospital. ¡Qué pequeño se ve el cuerpo cuando el alma lo abandona! Para ser el mes de junio, el cuarto del hospital se sentía frío. Mi tata no llevaba ni dos horas de muerto y se podía sentir como se enfriaba rápidamente el cuerpo.

En el cuarto nos encontrábamos solamente mujeres: mi nana, mi madre, hermanas, tías y primas; todas llorando y acariciando el cuerpo de mi tata. Mi nana le sostenía la mano, mi tía Rosa le tocaba la cara y mi hermana Luisa lloraba a sus pies. A nosotras nos tocaba lamentar por el difunto. Entre tanto mis padres y mis tíos tenían que arreglar detalles importantes, tales como conseguir ropa en que enterrar a mi tata y hacer los preparativos para el inesperado funeral. Todo se tenía que hacer con rapidez, ya que el calor del desierto descompone rápidamente el cuerpo. En menos de 24 horas mi tata estaría enterrado.

Su muerte en verdad fue inesperada, ya que siempre fue un hombre recio. La sufrida vida de vaquero por lo menos eso le había dejado como pensión en su vejez: un cuerpo maltratado, pero sano. Era hombre de pueblo, acostumbrado a la lucha. De pequeño sobrevivió la Revolución de 1910, de joven luchó contra los indios Yaquis y de viejo conquistó el desierto de Sonora, logrando que las áridas tierras produjeran trigo y mantuvieran ganado. Aun con sus 76 años de edad, mi tata ensillaba su caballo o iba a buscar ganado en el monte. Si se le hacía tarde, no dudaba en tirar su cobija en la vil piedra para pasar la noche.

Es por eso que cuando llegaron las noticias de que mi tata se encontraba en el hospital, la familia no se consternó mucho. El sufría de un simple dolor en el pecho, causado probablemente por la falta de descanso. Tan seguros estaban mis tíos de su prognóstico, que no querían decirle a mi nana que su esposo estaba internado. No querían alarmarla.

Para mi pobre nana, la vida como esposa de vaquero y madre de siete hijos, no fue tan benévola. Al pasar los años, la preocupación y el reumatismo la fueron lentamente destruyendo. Solamente quedaba la sombra de aquella mujer que respaldó a mi abuelo en sus victorias. Una sombra deformada por las reumas y sentenciada a pasar todo el día en una silla de ruedas.

Mi madre pensó que era una injusticia no decirle a mi nana que su esposo estaba internado. Mi madre es una de aquellas personas con un sexto sentido que le permite ver el futuro, pero sin la habilidad para cambiarlo. Sus instintos le advertían de la segura muerte de mi tata. Sabía que mi nana tenía el derecho de ver a su esposo por última vez, pero nadie la escuchaba. La acusaban de "escandalosa", diciendo que sólo mortificaría a mi nana. Al fin y al cabo en dos días se esperaba que mi tata saliera del hospital.

Pero mi madre, que es fuerte de carácter, no desistía, y de tanto insistir, mis tíos empezaron a dudar. Mi nana nunca los perdonaría si algo le pasase a mi tata. Bajo esta amenaza y las constantes insistencias de mi madre, mis tíos decidieron mentirle a mi nana. Le dijeron que su esposo estaba internado con un simple resfriado. Al recibir las noticias, mi nana suplicó que la llevaran inmediatamente al hospital. Mis familiares, preocupados por su delicada salud, la llevaron de mala gana.

La visita al hospital fue uno de esos pequeños milagros que hace la vida tan maravillosa. Parecía un evento sin importancia, mi nana en su silla de ruedas y mi tata acostado. Entre las sábanas de la cama estaban escondidas las marchitas manos de ambos, sus dedos entrelazados. Pasaban largos minutos sin que ninguno de los dos dijese algo. Después de 53 años de casados, a lo mejor no tenían nada nuevo que decirse. O tal vez, después de tanto tiempo juntos, la voz dejaba de ser la forma más efectiva de comunicación. Por media hora ambos disfrutaron de su compañía y se veían verdaderamente felices.

Cuando llegó el momento de marchar, mi nana sonrojando pidió a mis padres que la levantaran y la acercaran más a mi tata. Quería darle un beso de despedida. Mis padres extrañados acedieron, ya que mis abuelos nunca habían demostrado afecto tan abiertamente ante sus hijos. Mis abuelos eran gente del desierto, donde la sequedad del suelo se reflejaba en la aridez de los sentimientos. Pero este pequeño beso, puesto en el arrugado cachete de mi tata, iba cargado de muchos años de amor y devoción. A los dos les brillaban los ojos como si de nuevo fueran novios. Mi tata se ruborizó y mi nana sonreía.

Son pocos los que tienen la fortuna de tener la última despedida. La segunda vez que volvió mi nana a ese cuarto, mi tata ya estaba envuelto en las sábanas verdes del hospital. . . .

The Raza Who Scored Big in Anáhuac

Gary D. Keller,
El Huitlacoche

I thought, being raza, that this was my tierra. You know, roots, ¡qué sé yo! Now I think maybe I'm just another extranjero, one who crossed the wrong-way river.

I came down to learn stuff. Junior term in Anáhuac. At the Universidad Nacional Autónoma—the student movement—¡la revolución estudiantil!—I met and befriended Felipe Espinoso. He helped me with my notes because, speaking frankly, my written castellano isn't the best. "Language loss" is what some professor once muttered to me when I tested out at Cal State. Felipe was curious about Chicano ways. He called me "güero valín, the Mexican in preppie polo shirts." That made me laugh and I would kid him about the same Yucatecan guayabera that he wore every day that I knew him. We were both attending the same course, Theory and Practice of Mexican Social Class Structure, taught by tal profesor, one Maximiliano Peón, who alerted us at once to the fact that even though his remuneration was not enough to cover the gasoline that the trip cost him, he was proud to be teaching this course at UNAM as a servicio to the youth of his patria.

From the profile Felipe reminded me—it was an uncanny, almost perfect likeness—of a Mayan head in Palenque, a bas-relief with the prominent Mayan nose and receding forehead that I had pondered over in an art book at the Cal library. I had always wanted urgently to visit Palenque. I used to think about its gothic arches and cornstalk glyphs when I was just a kid, working behind the counter at the Taco Bell, baking cinnamon crispas. Now I found myself in Anáhuac, peering into the eyes of a Maya.

Felipe pressed me hard on Aztlán, and pleased with his avid interest, I was proud to tell him about the meaning of César Chávez's black águila in a white circle, of vato and cholo, the Sleepy Lagoon riots, the finer points of pachuquismo, the fate of Reies Tijerina, the difference between an acto and a mito, Los Angeles street murals, and the old Operation Wetback of the '50s and the silly Tortilla Curtain que parió.

In turn, I queried him about the political peripecias of Vicente Lombardo Toledano, the pastimes of Siqueiros when they threw him in the Lecumberri lockup, the subtleties redounding in the national diversion of deciphering every six years who the PRI tapado really was, the new malinchista movement of contemporary Mexican feministas, what Buñuel had really meant in *Los olvidados*, and why Cantinflas had plastic surgery done on his notable nose.

One afternoon after class, at the tortería which surely has the best crema in the valley of Mexico, La Tortería Isabela la Católica, only a few minutes from the University library which is a living historico-revolutionary mural, I confided in him a Chicano hope for a bina-tional carnalismo. We were both brought to tears and to a heartfelt abrazo de correligionarios, not to mention compinches.

In class Felipe Espinoso was quiescent. Weren't we all? In our aula there were over 80 where there should have been 50. The earliest got seats, the next earliest, window sills, then came those who pressed along the walls until the door could no longer be opened and the half dozen hapless laggards who either missed the lecture of the day or tried to catch a semblance of the proceedings from outside, through a window. The University had been built for 120,000 almas; there were over 260,000 in attendance. Classes had been scheduled seven days a week from the earliest morning until midnight.

During the days approaching registration, Indians trod in from the valley, from the mountains surrounding the valley, from the plains beyond the mountains surrounding the valley, from the plains beyond the mountains which circle this Anáhuac. They filed down the mountain roads, dog-tired, without chavos or any other material resources, spurred on by an implacable will for wisdom and upward mobility. Alentados perhaps by rural maestras de escuela they came for the term to UNAM where tuition was basically free. They tra-veled the roads in huaraches made from the rubber of discarded tires, slept where they could, in attics, hidden in obscure recintos of the university, in the swimming pool when there was no water, waited resignedly for a seat to study in the hopeless library that could no longer accommodate the push of the masses, begged or hustled for the term's nourishment. I have seen this drive that cannot be stemmed by any earthly privation or police state curtain at my heartfelt border, across which God's innocent children slip into the promised coloso of milk and miel, and I genuflect before these campesino multitudes and each day relive their fierce, steadfast resolve, share their dusty anger, revere their pursuit of self-improvement.

Halfway into the course, Felipe made a pronouncement. "Güero, I thought I liked Prof. Maximiliano Peón. I no longer like him. He is a deception. He is pequeño burgués."

"He comes out here for nothing to teach this unwashed horde and untouched rabble, doesn't he?"

"Sure, he comes out, and punctually. He's all subjectivity and nineteenth-century retórica, spouting about the incontrovertible objective realities of Marxist-Leninist revolutionary materialism. He's a living contradiction, a comfortable gentilhombre, an hidalgo of the professorate, all immersed in bourgeois pieties and comforts, drunk with arriviste parfums and amaretto and frangelico liqueurs. But to assuage his sotted, corrupted soul, to aggrandize his smug persona, to allay his midnight anxieties—because he knows well that his kind and his class would be first to the paredón in a genuine revolution—he sacrifices salary and comes out here to provoke Inditos de Lerdo Chiquito so that they may march to revolutionary beats, so that they may be mowed down by imported burp guns. Yes, he'll watch it all on his Magnavox in the parlor. He'll be hoping that he's hedged every bet, that he'll come out triumphant no matter who wins the partido."

I should confess now that Felipe was a fanatic for the jai alai and he had taught me to be a fanatic. His frontón imagery troubled me. Of course it was what everybody tried to do at the jai alai, bet on the underdog when the price was low and hope for the score to turn, then bet again on the opposing team at good odds and sit out the game a sure winner no matter which team won. . . . I protested, "But I love his Spanish! My God, his command of language!"

"¡Coño! Sure you do. You're a poor, hapless Chicano—a güero pocho boy who has never had the opportunity to study your mother tongue with any formality or system until now. Don't be deceived. It's all Porfirian sophistry and pedagogical pettifoggery. He doesn't even speak Spanish anyway. He speaks Castilian. And these poor, ingenuous indios—I include myself here, once a poor simpleton from Quintana Roo—who also are mostly tonguesmen of Zapoteca, Huichol, or whatever, they are mesmerized by the castizo buffoon who wishes to provoke their action for lost causes so he can feel assuaged for having 'done something about the Mexican social class problem.'

"This is wrong," he went on. "Let us have a revolution in Olmeca, or Chichimeca, or Náhuatl even, or Mayaquiché. Anything but the Porfirian castellano of the Mexican empire and the simpering sleight of hand of the crypto-revolutionary."

So, then, Maximiliano fell from his pedestal. But who or what to replace him with?

The Virgin of Guadalupe's day was approaching. We were tertuliando with other left-leaning student intellects at a café in the slanting sun on the Promenade of Institutionalized Revolution, near the cathedral. We could see a pilgrimage approaching like marabunta down the wide promenade. Felipe told me that tonight would be a fine one to be at the jai alai. Probably he should take all my money and his too and bet it on the main partido.

"Why is that, Felipe?"

He turned to the promenade. "They will be betting heavy." The pilgrimage swept down the promenade, eighteen campesinos abreast, marching in for the novena. There were delegations from Tenancingo and Tlaxcala, Acámbaro and Acatlán, Pátzcuaro and Pachuca, and even Pénjamo and Tzintzuntzan. First the crests of cyclists congruous to paramilitants. They had plastic virgins tacked to their handlebars and wheels and pennants that saluted the breeze of their own making. Then came legions of dusty benditos, huffing and chanting the Ave María, each village headed by a priest and an icon. Then down the Promenade of Institutionalized Revolution came herds of goats and turkeys and aggressive geese, bullied by trotting boys and mongrels. The peddlers followed too, hawking tostadas in green or red sauce, sweet potatoes in carts with piercing steam whistles, guava and cajeta, mamey and mango ice, jícama in vinaigrette. Jesting and cursing in the militant sun, the pilgrims marched and peeled corn husks, smearing the tender grain of their elotes with colored sauce. On the special earthen track, the last kilometer to the cathedral doors, the supplicants came by on bloody knees, bearing the indrawn vision. In the courtyard they were doing Amerindian dances against the slanting, sinking cathedral walls. Precisely every ten meters hung white metal signs with red letters neatly stenciled: It is strictly forbidden to urinate against these holy walls.

That night at the jai alai with all our funds in hand I worried and became a little drunk. Felipe doubted too and wondered if we oughtn't be at the cockfights. "On nights of the novena, the Indians come to the cock arena and wager nuggets of gold that they have dug out of the countryside."

"But here too the galleries are filled with countryfolk. Besides, Felipe, we are fanatics for the jai alai. We know nothing of cockfights."

"True enough. All I know of the cocks is that they use one straight and one curved dagger. That's all I know. It's a question of breeders and other intimate variables." Felipe sighed. "Whatever happens tonight, we cast our lot with the people."

"Sure," I said. Right then I felt muy raza, muy Mexican. "Sí, con el pueblo." But immediately I started to wonder. "Do you think the games are fixed?"

"Who would fix them for the poor to win?"

"Maybe the government. On orders of the authority."

"I wouldn't put that beyond the authorities. A devious scheme to enervate the pilgrims. But no. Why should the government subsidize the gambling vice? Besides, it doesn't happen all the time. It's just . . . a pattern. We must realize that by probability we stand to lose. But the odds make it worthwhile. A handsome wager."

"But I don't want to lose, Felipe. If I lose I will have to eat pinto beans all month. I'll have to return to Califas."

Felipe laughed. "Come now, compis. It's not every day that a vato loco can wager with the people with a firm hand. Maybe the match is fixed every night before the pilgrims make the final march to celebrate Tepeyac. Just to brighten the Indian's firm belief in the miraculous. But no, I don't think there's any question of a fixed game. It's simply the milieu, those days when the campo and the aldea come to court, the Indians packed in the galleries, hiding behind masks. I think it's a spirit that descends on the jai alai court. An ether which comes from the galleries and penetrates the players."

"Perhaps a revolutionary spirit?"

"Yes, but lapped up by the gambling vice the way mole is contained and dammed by corn dough. The inditos make their way up to the galleries expecting the supernatural."

I laughed. "What would Gramsci think of this, Pablo Freire, even the barbudo Carlos Marx? Could they construct a paradigm pa'l fenómeno?"

"Hard to say. It's too early in the course."

"You're right, Felipe. On a night like tonight one should be a jai alai fanatic. Have you seen all the grenaderos about?"

"Yes. They've even brought a contingent in from Atzcapotzalco. I'm sure there are two in front of every pulquería, every brothel, every revolutionary square, every Ateneo in Mexico City."

"How many do you think there are at the University library, underneath the mural?"

Saturday night at the Palacio de la Pelota, El Frontón México. The jai alai court was stretched and wide, bounded by three rock walls. The open end was strung with an immense steel net protecting the spectators from the missiles. Occupying the choice seats in the middle of the stands were the vested ones, Arabs and Jews, gachupines and wealthy Mexicans who played the favorite and lapped up the chiquitero money.

There was a roar from the crowd. The intendant and four huge Basques with long straw wickers bound to their wrists entered the court. They marched single file and solemnly along the wood boundary line. Then they turned and faced the crowd, placed their wickers across their hearts in salute, and gave the slightest of nods. There were whistles, jeers, and enthusiastic applause. The players broke rank and began to practice up. It was two mean frisky bucks playing against two stooping esthetes.

Felipe studied the program. "This match is a timeless syndrome: youth versus experience. Only a poet or saint will win this."

"Well then," I asked, "who do we bet on?"

"It doesn't matter, güero. The team that falls behind and permits the chiquiteros to bet their pittances. We will bet on the underdog, the people, and their expectations for a miracle."

"I like that, Felipe. A higher logic. I may be a vato loco, but you are a vate loco. A meta-wager and a melodrama. A dialectic that ends in a materialistic. I like the pastel money of México. It's easier than the hardened green of the dólar."

Redcaps called the odds out, which were an even 100 red versus 100 blue, and the match to 30 points began. The fierce bucks dominated from the very start, and as the score mounted in their favor the odds dwindled, 50, 30, 10 to 100. From the galleries there was a steady projection of sullen mirth.

I saw an Olmec-looking type call out, "That old camel should be playing marbles with his grandchild!" and a striking mestizo who looked the prototype of Vasconcelos's raza cósmica imprecated a few times and then said, "Get him a pair of roller skates . . . and a Seeing Eye dog!" Rejoined a weasel who looked more like the critics of Vasconcelos who coined a raza cómica, "No, old fool!" Bring him Sancho Panza!"

The score was 20 to 12. The redcaps had become bored and sat in the aisles kibitzing with their clients. The guards, instead of standing straight up, were lounging on the very net that bounded the court. And the sharks filed their teeth or counted their fistfuls of wagers on short odds or nonchalantly cracked sunflower seeds. That was when we bet most of the money credited to us for a month of studies and livelihood on the underdog at 80 to 1000. The sharks were glad to take our money. "No lo hagan," a concerned bourgeois gentilhomme advised us. "You're just going to make a tiburón happy. ¡Que el partido se va de calle!"

A portentous occurrence. The jai alai became like the opera buffa. The old artistes made two points and there was an ominous silence. The redcaps got up from the aisles but called out a few odds. There was almost no betting. They were waiting—the galleries and the short money, seven, eight thousand strong—for another mysterium. The intereses creados squirmed up in their chairs like weasels. This point—it was taking too long, too many volleys! The great and turning point came in like high tide and the redcaps quieted nor scuffles nor coughs, but the pok of the rubber and rocklike sphere impacted and spread upon the front wall and the long, retrograde arc of the orb obfuscating in spotlights, the skim of wrists along the green middling, and the crack of stone's conjunction with straw. Rolando, the stiff yet still graceful elder, scooped up the ball on the short hop and propelled it swan's neck thick on the middle so it angled sinuously on the low, wide front, bounced within the far outside wood, and spiraled into the netting. The galleries were ripped wide open with Amerindian joie de vivre. The men or beasts within tore asunder their poses and stepped outside themselves. The promised sign! I turned to Felipe. He glowed with cherubic ecstasy. I held his head like a son. The redcaps called out odds: 40 to 100, make it 45, no, 50 to 100. Red and blue tickets passed countless brown hands. The aisles writhed like serpents. We bore the manic coaster to allegorical heaven.

It was like the Westerns, too. The well-off villains in their business suits and gold pocket watches presenced their reserved finale. They put away their pepitas and pistachios and their eyes popped and their jaws hung awry. "Cover!" they begged the redcaps. They wanted to cover, to hedge. The God-fearing rested easy. None of us doubted the outcome. Social and poetic justice would be done.

Rolando was all about, luxuriating in his renaissance, his regained nerve.

Soon we were winning! The young bucks leaned against the wall and slowly sank to the floor, their innards chafing, their tongues flapping. Holding his wicker high above him like a torch, Rolando traversed the court with the stately mockery of a ceremonious bull-fighter. Caught up in the euphoria I began to scream a confused litany of mythic templates. The eagle, the serpent, the nopal, the thunder-bird, the ¡Sí se puede!, la MECHA, el Anáhuac, Aztlán, all jumbled in the same olla. Felipe and I embraced. "¡Vamos a ganar! ¡Venceremos!"

Then, an inexplicable alteration of events. The elders loosened up —¡que se aflojaron!—got tired, and permitted the youngsters to come back. The game tied up at 29. The ultimate metaphysic! Peepee was drawn from the caved-in bladders of many. The galleries lost their nerve and hastened to hedge their spleens. The sharks and business-men, anxious to reduce their losses, covered the Indians and bet all the Rolando they could. The redcaps shrieked out the odds: 100 even, 100 pesos, pick'em.

I grabbed Felipe. "Los indios have lost their nerve and are seeking insurance. ¡Tienen los huevos en la garganta!"

"Me too!"

"Let's cover! If we do, we win either way!"

"No way," Felipe said, "let us ride!"

I was in a swoon. "Oh, God! All that pastel!"

"Are you with me?"

I squeezed his hand. My knees were buckling. His face was mauve and bloated. "God, yes!"

I am an innocent, I thought. The ingenuous fanatic. For the moment I loved him so, I could have given him my life.

The ultimate point began.

Rolando served the ball, a giveaway straight to the opposing frontman. We should have lost, instead the ball dribbled obscenely out of the unnerved wicker.

"We won!"

The young buck climbed and clawed the net in a twist of fury. Futile as Bergman's squire.

I turned to Felipe. "You won! You knew the old boy'd do it!"

He didn't seem terribly happy, though. He pointed at Rolando leaving for the dressing room, wiping his brow amid hosannas. "It took a lot out of him."

I felt funny. Felipe and I split the money, 50-50. The devalued pastel wad of Mexican money barely entered my pocket. I had more in the wallet. There were bills in my shirt pocket. Child supplicants stood willfully at the exit next to the Palacio. I emptied coins into each calloused hand.

"Don't do that," he said.

"Why not?"

"It's bad form. It makes you look like a gringo."

"I know that. It's only because tonight I've scored big."

"No, never. You'll spoil them."

To win money: that was not enough. Felipe was still angry, knotted up by the match, and slowly I became angry too. It was not enough on the eve of the Virgin's day, despite the magnificent catharsis. Why? No más por no más.

Felipe had been silent while we lined up and collected our bets. Now he almost whined. "Now we must go and fuck some woman. I know a brothel, not too far."

"I don't want to fuck some woman! I'm too buoyant. I want to keep my money. Not tonight, Felipe. I'm too worn."

"Pues sí, compis. That's the way we do things here. The night won't be complete. El rito del jai alai se lo exige."

"I thought you were a poet, a mystic, and a left-leaning intellectual."

Felipe cursed a lot about shitting in the milk of the Virgin and all that folklore. "If you win, you've got to go. Don't leave me to my designs."

"What's this brothel like?"

"Perverse! What güero can claim to have known México without having visited its muchachas?"

"What do you mean, perverse?" I asked him hostilely.

He grinned. "Authentically perverse."

La Madama Lulú's was not perverse. It was repulsive, y me pareció muy típico. Two grenaderos sat on the sidewalk in front of the brothel. Some político or máximo chingón was fucking his brains out. Their carbines lay on the pavement at their sides. They winked at us as we went in. The brothel bureaucrats sat us on an overstuffed Louis XVI and the whores lined up and flaunted us all petite soirée fête in stained miniskirts. "¡Vamos a hacer beibis!"

I didn't have the huevos to choose, so the most entrepreneurial of their lot plopped on my thighs and fondled my member. Soon, having been kneaded like a croissant, it began to acquire that mauve, belligerent feel. "Ven aquí," she coaxed. She took some of my salmon and sandía-colored money and gave it to the bookkeeper. The bookkeeper gave me a red poker chip. Then I had to give the poker chip to the porter, who meticulously opened the door to a broomcloset cubicle and handed me a roll of toilet paper. We went inside. I didn't give a shit anymore. ¡Qué carajos! I was resolved. Yet suddenly I realized I was fucking a perfect stranger.

Later we were famished. The high was worn and it had turned cold and raw. There were pilgrims wandering the street, like strays. Felipe and I went into an all-night estancia where they cut newspapers into napkins. We had steaming hot caldo tlalpeño. We had machitos, finely minced tacos of bull testicles sprinkled with aguacate and cilantro in piquant sauce; sympathetic cannibalism. We washed it down with Carta Blanca. Felipe was quiet and grave. He looked frightened. I couldn't fathom what he was thinking.

I kept drinking. After a while I asked him, "Why don't men and women do anything or go anywhere together in this country? Why are the men in the plaza and the women en casa?"

"They do go out together," he protested.

"Sure, to a té danzante at five in the afternoon."

"Those are appropriate hours. I'm sorry that we are not as advanced as your civilization."

"I've told you before, Felipe, it's not my civilization. Shit, I just live there. Don't blame me you sent out a fuck-up like Santa Anna to do an hombre's job."

"Here we still believe in the novia santa."

"You do?"

"Sure."

"I mean you, Felipe Espinoso from Quintana Roo."

"Why not?"

"It seems muy raro. I bet. The novia santa. It goes well with la casa chica."

"Don't insult me."

"I'm sorry. You have a novia waiting for you?"

"Sure."

"Where?"

"In Tulúm. It's small."

"Sure, I know it. There are ruins there. Hay presencia del pasado."

"Tienes razón."

"And how long since you've seen her?"

"The six years I've been here at the University. I take a course and a course and a course. Como tu work-study, right?"

"Not quite. You're going to marry her?"

"As soon as I graduate."

The night was cool and Mexican. Stars appeared like wishes. It was very still, soon it would be early. We walked with our hands in our pockets and our faces down, steadfast in the drunken ambience. We came to a park. The coconuts and the palms were still and etched. Some campesinos with no place to go were trying to sleep on the benches that they had arrogated. There was suddenly a clump of grass in front of me. I plopped on it. The grass tickled my nostrils. I giggled.

"Get up!" Felipe sounded alarmed. He pulled me. It seemed like someone else's arm.

"¡Viva la revolución!"

"Be quiet, won't you!"

"What do you mean, quiet? Is this a police state? ¡Viva la revolución! ¡Viva la virgen de Tepeyac! ¡Viva Tontantzín! Let every good fellow now join in this song, Vive la companie. Good health to each other and pass it along, vive la companie."

"Get up!"

"No, you come down. Down to my level."

"All right. If you quiet down."

I laughed. "Where I live they say Mexicans—that means Chicanos of course, not you real Mexicans—were made to pizcar tomates because they're built low to the ground. What do you think about that?"

He flashed his winning grin. "I'm curious about your Chicano ways."

"Well. When are you going to graduate?"

"Soon, if you keep quiet so no one steals my money tonight."

"Did you walk to Mexico City from Tulúm?"

"Well, no. Actually, I got an aventón."

"And were you like the indios that come streaming in from the picos and the valles around registration time?"

"Most assuredly."

"And did you live like them, begging, and hustling, and working?"

He smiled. "Well, nobody gets to find much work in this city."

"So then?"

"So I'm still hustling. Only I'm an advanced student now, senior class."

"¿Qué me dices?"

"I'm sorry, güero. We were playing only with your pastel money."

"Only my money? But I saw you pitch in your share."

"That was merely sleight of hand."

"I see. So then, at 29 up, you weren't really that nervous."

"Oh, I was very nervous."

"Yeah, but not as nervous as me."

"No, I wouldn't think so."

"No, you wouldn't think so. After all, for you it was win or tie."

"Something like that."

"And you don't feel bad?"

"I feel very bad. I need for you to know how bad I feel, even now, after winning, despite winning. Not only the money, but my life's dream, enough to live on so that I can take a full course of study and graduate. Porque, compis, tú eres mi cuate, ¿sabes? O, como dicen los tuyos, soy tu carnal."

"How can you say this shit to me now? Do you know I'm debating whether or not to kick your fucking head in?"

"Pues, ponte chango, carnal. Pa' la próxima más aguzao, vato. Porque ya aprendiste. That's what Buñuel meant in *Los olvidados*. Like they say in these parts, más cornadas da el hambre que el toro."

"Don't hand me that pestilent shit. You simply hustled me. I'm just as poor as you. You knew if I lost that match I would probably have had to drop out and return home. Either that or starve."

"And you're not used to starving. Sure you're poor—I realize that. But you work. As a stock boy, at Taco Bell, as a piss-pot polisher. Lo que sea, entran los chavitos, haga cola para el financial aid. You're poor like Cheech and Chong. We use the same word, poor, but we don't mean the same referent. I mean devastated, a nullity without the remotest identity."

"Why are you telling me all this stuff now? You won your ticket. Why couldn't you have just let me keep on thinking you were a fucking prince?"

"Pues, por pura vergüenza. You may not believe it: allí en la casa de putas, where much profound Mexican thought takes form, I thought about it long and hard. But you deserve more. You are a fine fellow, very young, ingenuo, and my sense of shame and your need to know, they joined forces. It may not be as pretty as pastel illusions or the half-breed Virgin who showed herself to the cosmic race, but I felt I owed you the truth. Por eso bajaste al Anáhuac, ¿no ?"

"And besides, you have enough money now, ¿verdad? You've got your graduation ticket and you can give up your contingency pigeon, right?"

He looked crestfallen. "I'm sorry. Los malos hábitos are difficult to overcome. I want to go to school intensively now and graduate and no longer do what I used to have to do."

"Well, I guess the course is over. It's been . . . well, it's definitely been a learning experience."

"Get up, güero, please."

"Why should I? I want to sleep. Here, entre las palmas."

"They won't let you sleep here. Some grenaderos will come by. They'll take you to the station and keep the pastel money which you think is so much softer than the dollar."

The grass began to smell of manure. I got up.

On the ninth day I discovered I had contracted the gonk. That was quite a letdown. The same day the pilgrims returned to the countryside and the grenaderos abandoned the University library with its revolutionary mural. I watched the campesinos as they trod out of the capital. The drunken revel was over and so was the holy fervor. They were tired, broke, bearing loathsome lesions on their knees that peered out of their trousers, which had worn away in their penitent sojourn in the Virgin's sanctuary. They looked like a crest-fallen army in retreat. They resembled those Vietnamese multitudes on the run that we used to look at, guilt-ridden and repulsed, on the evening news.

When the last of the campesinos and their geese had moved on I could then cross the Promenade of Institutionalized Revolution to the barrio pharmacy where they were caring for me. All my money seemed to be dissipating in penicillin and in little luxuries to assuage the discomfort. Every day I walked sore and open-legged to the pharmacy and pulled down my trousers in the back room. The attendant, una celestina fea y arrugada who looked like the incarnation of gleeful disapproval, would put the needle in.

"How many cc's are you going to give me?"

"You need a million cc's this time up."

"No chingues. You'll have the needle in my bun for over five minutes. It'll be an hour before I'll be able to move my leg."

"¡Cómo que no chingues! That's what *you* should say to yourself, güerito. ¡Porque chingue y chingue y mira el resultado! O como decimos por aquí: Quien se acuesta con pulgas . . ."

"Spare me the dénouement. Let's get it over with. Look, why don't you just give me 500,000?"

"You want 500,000? I'll give it! You know how many machos come back here three weeks later, open-legged and bawling because the pus is back again and dripping out of their putrid chiles?"

"God no, give me the million. Anything."

"Here it goes, y no chilles, ¿eh? güerito valín. Porque como sabes, tú tienes la enfermedad de los meros machos." She began to laugh with great moral gusto. As my leg turned numb I realized that in Mexico the man wasn't always in the plaza and the woman only en casa.

It was just a few days before my term was up and I was to return to Califas. I bumped into Espinoso in the library.

"Hola, vate loco."

He looked embarrassed, almost searching for a space to slink into. "Hola, vate loco. It's been some days since I've seen you."

"Well, yes, I've been spending time at the old farmacia. I got the gonk, thanks to you and your macho ideas and your disgusting putas that you believe are sensuously perverse."

"Well, I figured. I got it too. La mierda de gonorrea is epidemic here."

"Well, that's the best fucking news I've heard all week!"

"You think so? You want to reenact the Alamo here in the library? Fuck it, man, be happy it's just gonk que se quita con penicilina and not what they say you get on the other side of the river, herpes. Let me tell you something, güero, and this is God's truth. Since I've been here, six years in this hostile valley, that was the first time I got laid."

"Not enough billetiza, right?"

"Right. It wasn't a financial priority."

"Sure, you didn't have a sufficiently dumb gringo to hustle big enough at the jai alai. Well, you must be busted by now what with shots and poultices and all. Here, let me stake you again—what the fuck, the Chicano baboso never learns." I flipped out a pink and canary bill with the likeness of Venustiano Carranza and stuffed it in his guayabera pocket.

"I'll accept it as a wedding present on behalf of my novia and me."

"Yeah. I was sure that you'd accept it o.k., Mr. Savoir Faire."

"I don't mean to hurt you, güero valín. But, ¿sabes lo que tú eres . . . en el fondo?"

"No, Mr. Maya. No idea what I am en el fondo. But I'm sure you're gonna tell me, Mr. Sabelotodo."

"En el fondo tú eres . . . ¡turista!"

Time softens the sense of injury and lets the little nostalgias form the veins and lodes that make the past palatable. If I had an address to write to, I would have sent him a card or something. But there was no address, maybe the empty swimming pool, o como dijo esa noche, una nulidad sin identidad remota, and barring that I would find myself in the State library, which seemed like an unsullied cavern, to sit and ponder, open the page in the art book to the Palenque man, frame ideas, sometimes talk silently to the stone head.

When you give meaningful events the profound reflection that they require, the many details that you missed in the ongoing come into relief and give a new bent to the hurt. In the labyrinthine library of my soledad I uncovered and relived the discreet portents and signs. How he envied and admired attributes that I didn't remotely realize. Güero, he called me, though in this country I could not remotely pass for fair. And my blue jeans and knitted polo shirt were such a center of attraction, the ballpoint pen that contained three cartridges, red, black, and green. Finally, I gave it to him. The way he liked to introduce me to girls on the campus—girls, I conclude now, who were not his friendly acquaintances as I had thought at the time, but barely accorded him the minimal courtesies of fellow studenthood. He would introduce me, I realize now, with a touch of the panderer, and how they would take to the exotic Chicano, the güero valín with a rather hairy chest who maybe reminded them in his knit shirt of some phantasm image they had conjured in their head, a Robert Redford, well-heeled, privileged and native in Spanish. You were waiting there, Felipe, furious and sotted with envy, bridling your lust—how you must have kept so much venom under wraps—hoping that I would puncture the maiden ethics of niñas bien, maybe score, maybe there would be a scrap of carrion in it for you. For you hadn't been laid in six years!

How you queried me, Maya, about so many things like routes and rivers, fences and sensors, coyotes and pollos. Were you trying on Chicano, my friend? Were you speculating on the North? How proud you were, como un tío paternal, when you arranged a little public trial for me at the tortería, bade me eat the chile más pequín de la tortería. And when I passed your little test and won a round of student applause, did you not say, "See, he's no gringo now, he's earned his bones." But it was nothing! I've been eating those pequines my whole life!

Now I feel so mortified that I could have confided in you—¿qué?—after two or three days of acquaintanceship at most, such intimate yearnings as my whole carnal hope for Mexican-Chicano compañerismo. ¡Qué ingenuo! Now I know, máximo peón, that even in oppression, even if there are only two oppressed peas in a con-stricted pod, they will disaggregate into an oppressor and an oppressed, a siervo and a señor, a leader and a led. That is the nature of oppression and of the oppressed, the theory and the practice. That they know only what they know and act on what they know, a great chain of oppressed people, a great daisy chain of being that leads not straight to St. Thomas's sandía-hued heaven, but low, up and down picos, down and up valleys, across llanos and even across rivers where the current runs in opposing directions. Yet, truly escarmentado that I am for having so readily and unselfconsciously confided in El Otro, that moment in the tortería, that heartfelt abrazo over tortas de lomo . . . How is it that two oprimidos of such divergent estirpes, of such varied formation, could have, if just for a transitory term, communed? I cherish that shared governance of perceptions even though to obtain it requires a racking sojourn into memories filled with penitence and humiliation. And I think of a passage in Heming-way where it is observed that where we are weak, there where nature surely breaks us, and if we fare with good fortune, and go on the mend, there where we were weak we are now the strongest. And although in the end it's all the same for nature will break us, definitively, it will not be at the junction where once we were weak and now we are strong.

Amigo, I don't quarrel with your many truths or the intensity of your motives. Of one thing, no cabe duda, I am poor like Cheech and Chong—thank God for it, bless that level of poverty that still subsidizes the notion of humorous solutions.

Well, yes, there is one perception that I quarrel with. ¡Yo no soy turista! In truth you were the tourist, amigo, as well as the tour guide and the conning lout. A most engaging and eager one, the way you genuinely investigated my nature, but like any tourist, even an enlightened and avid one, you compared the landscape by a self-same standard. Your sense of the picturesque, the empathetic, and the offensive were all measured out in the same pastel currency. But the estranged is different from the tourist. It is his lot to wander forth, to cross rivers that flow up course, seek out his own image in the dubious landscape of the other, search for a currency that isn't there. Por supuesto, the Chicano needs to gaze into smoky mirrors that reflect no peer. Know this, venerable Maya head that has perdured for 1200 years on a coated ivory page in a slick art book in a State library: I am strong where I've been broken and I'm not prepared to cave in.

Acknowledgments

Director, 1983-84:	Héctor Orjuela
Coordinators:	Estela M. Muñoz
	María Almanzo
Director, 1984-85:	Julian Palley
Coordinators:	Ivonne Gordon Vailakis
	Christina Rhemm

Judges

Faculty:
Alejandro Morales
María Herrera-Sobek
Anne Cruz
Seymour Menton

External Judges:
José Monleón
Linda Fregoso
Margarita Cota-Cárdenas
Jorge Mariscal
Gustavo Segade
Marta Sánchez
Rosaura Sánchez
Francisco Jiménez
Guadalupe Valdés
Armando Migueles
Justo Alarcón
Porfirio Sánchez

126

Readers:

Guillermo Retana
Juliana Anzellini
Alicia Churchill
Elizabeth Báez
María del Rosario González
María Teresa Marrero
Magdalena Andrade
Juan Manuel Bernal
Ivonne Gordon Vailakis

The Department of Spanish and Portuguese is grateful to the following for their help and encouragement:

Chancellor Jack Peltason
Chancellor Daniel Aldrich
Vice Chancellor William J. Lillyman
Dean Kendall Bailes
Dean Terence Parsons
Affirmative Action Officer Carla Espinoza
EOP Officer Manuel Gómez
Professor Eloy Rodríguez, Director,
    International Chicano Studies Program
Eric MacDonald, Librarian

Ex-Directors of the Contest:

Juan Villegas
Richard Barrutia

Literary Guild Members:

Tony Luna
Sylvia and Howard Lenhoff
Fred Flores
Rudolfo and Pat Anaya
Jeanne and Roy Giordano
Helen Johnson
Maricela Cortez Adams
Richard Barrutia

Billings and Swarez
Copper and Lybrand
Raymond del Río
O. B. Quijano, M.D.
Ronnie Reyes
Raymond Rangel
Silvas and Eaton
Alejandro Morales